Harry Harris is Group Chief Soccer Correspondent for the Mirror Group of Newspapers and was formerly with the *Daily Mail*, the *London Evening News* and the *Newcastle Journal*. He has collaborated on the autobiographies of several leading football managers and players, including Glenn Hoddle, Gary Mabbutt, Bill Nicholson and Terry Neill.

He had his wife Lesley have two children, Simon and Jordanna.

'MACCA CAN!'
THE STEVE McMAHON STORY

STEVE McMAHON
WITH HARRY HARRIS

FOREWORD BY GRAEME SOUNESS

PENGUIN BOOKS

PENGUIN BOOKS

Published by the Penguin Group
Penguin Books Ltd, 27 Wrights Lane, London W8 5TZ, England
Penguin Books USA Inc., 375 Hudson Street, New York, New York 10014, USA
Penguin Books Australia Ltd, Ringwood, Victoria, Australia
Penguin Books Canada Ltd, 10 Alcorn Avenue, Toronto, Ontario, Canada M4V 3B2
Penguin Books (NZ) Ltd, 182–190 Wairau Road, Auckland 10, New Zealand

Penguin Books Ltd, Registered Offices: Harmondsworth, Middlesex, England

First published by Pelham Books 1990
Published in Penguin Books 1991
1 3 5 7 9 10 8 6 4 2

Printed in England by Clays Ltd, St Ives plc

Contents

Foreword

by Graeme Souness
Manager, Rangers Football Club

I FIRST PLAYED AGAINST Steve McMahon when he was a young player with Everton Football Club. The first thing which struck me about him was his true competitiveness and he has now developed into the complete all-round footballer. He has the required aggression for the First Division and for International football and has a great ability for scoring goals.

Although not exactly the same in style, we do have certain similarities but I am certain Steve will score more goals in his career than I did during mine.

He epitomizes all that is best in British football and, in my opinion, he is now a truly world class footballer. I wish him every success in the future.

Introduction

by Harry Harris

STEVE McMAHON MADE SOCCER HISTORY at the end of the 1989–90 season as the only man to have captained both Merseyside clubs Everton and Liverpool. He was thrown the captain's armband towards the end of the match against QPR at Anfield, as Alan Hansen limped off, on the Saturday afternoon when Liverpool clinched their record 18th League Championship to beat off the challenge of runners-up Aston Villa with two games to spare. At the next match, a few days later, McMahon proudly led out the team, in the continued absence of injured club captain Alan Hansen, on the night Liverpool paraded the Barclays League Championship around Anfield. At the start of his career, McMahon earned the privilege of skippering Everton.

So, on 28 April 1990, McMahon wrote his name into the Hall of Fame as the first man to have skippered both Everton and Liverpool.

McMahon's life story is not only a fascinating insight into the secrets of Anfield, but he provides a behind the scenes view of the 1990 World Cup Finals in Italy. He reveals the rows, the mistakes as well as the bid for glory by England, the heartbreak of his mistake against the Republic of Ireland, and the confrontation with Bobby Robson when David Platt was chosen, at his expense, to play alongside Paul Gascoigne against West Germany in England's most important match since 1966.

England's World Cup campaign created enormous interest, with nearly 30 million TV viewers thrilled and, at the same time, devastated by the confrontation with West Germany. All the major decisions, all the drama, are vividly illustrated by McMahon's lucid account of events behind England's closed doors.

While McMahon's popular image is that of soccer's tough guy, he is actually a highly sensitive individual. He is the hard man of football with the soft centre. He seeks no sympathy when he's cut down in a combative midfield battle, and likewise he detests whingers who feign injury and exaggerate their pain. McMahon has succeeded the classic hard men of the past like Dave Mackay, Johnny Giles, Alan Ball and Norman Hunter. He has an abundance of skills as well as that determination to win the ball, an England international in a different league from the so-called hard men like anti-hero Vinny Jones.

However, off the field, there is a stunning contrast. He is a softly spoken gentleman, committed family man and a caring individual. His reaction to Hillsborough, the pain and anguish of the relatives of the bereaved and the survivors, revealed a man who had shared the nightmare of the ninety-five who died on the Leppings Lane terraces.

McMahon has the distinction of being Kenny Dalglish's first signing as manager of Liverpool. Kenny Dalglish urgently needed a *man* to replace Graeme Souness, who had been lured to Sampdoria in Italy. McMahon, a Merseysider, albeit an Evertonian, was the perfect replacement. The £350,000 paid to Aston Villa in 1985 now looks like one of the biggest give-aways of all time. It is put into perspective when Sampdoria themselves wanted McMahon to follow Souness and were willing to pay £2 million. Liverpool refused any overtures because there was no adequate replacement – even at £2 million!

His hero as a lad was Alan Ball. Ball, World Cup winner in 1966, is now a confirmed admirer of McMahon. Ball says:

> For me midfield is still the key area of football, and good midfield men make the game tick, they bring people into the game, keep the matches flowing and stamp their class into sides.
>
> It breaks my heart to see so many sides resort to the long ball, just pumping passes 50 yards. That's not how football was meant to be played. It's a sport of beauty and creativity. So many of today's midfield stars must bang their heads against a brick wall.

Ball, who starred for England, Everton, Arsenal and Southampton, before embarking into a career in management and coaching, was a firebrand, a ball of fire, an aggressive yet skilful midfield player on whom Sir Alf Ramsey relied as his engine-room to win the Jules Rimet trophy. Ball only has time for midfield players of passion and pride, and he says:

> Steve McMahon is the nearest thing to me I've seen in present-day football. I like the way he plays the game and, for me, he is the classic ball of fire. He works like hell in midfield, and when McMahon is playing well, Liverpool are firing on all cylinders. He has a heart as big as a bucket and dies for the cause.
>
> When the going gets tough, McMahon is in there earning the right to play his football. He'd be my first

choice in any club side. Steve is the cutting edge and engine-room rolled into one and makes Liverpool play. He also gets goals regularly. He seems to grow in stature when he runs out and is a vital man for their team.

It is easy to understand why Liverpool have signed McMahon on the longest contract of all the superstars at the club. McMahon, 29 in August 1990, signed a six-year deal in July 1989, which will take him to the end of his illustrious career at Anfield and will include a testimonial.

As Liverpool strode towards their seemingly impossible dream of League and Cup double after Hillsborough, England manager Bobby Robson said: 'McMahon was probably the most outstanding midfield player in the country at the end of that season. He was the force behind the Liverpool run towards the FA Cup and League Championship.'

As Liverpool chased the big prizes, inevitably once again, at the start of the new decade, Duncan McKenzie, once a talented forward with Leeds, Nottingham Forest and Everton, is convinced that McMahon has actually improved as he has matured. McKenzie, writing his regular column in a national newspaper, has no doubt that McMahon's powers are as formidable as ever. He wrote in *Today*: 'He is the unsung hero at Anfield. Great competitor. Now adding terrific running from deep positions to his battling, and has improved his finishing, too. Liverpool would find him hard to replace.'

On the eve of England embarking for the World Cup Finals, the most controversial debate centred around the midfield. Should Paul Gascoigne play? Can Neil Webb make it back from a damaged Achilles injury that sidelined him since September when he went down on World Cup duty in Sweden? It reached the stage where there was a campaign for the recall of Ray Wilkins at the age of 33, a veteran of the Mexico World Cup but who faded from the international scene after 1986 and his sending off against Morocco. Johnny Giles, 'the man the players read', according to his *Daily Express* column, came out totally in support of McMahon. He wrote:

> Bobby Charlton is the supreme example of a creative midfielder with genuine pace. Charlton could punish players by having the option of going by markers in the middle of the field. This, of course, gave his team a basic uncertainty in the opposition defences. Charlton could bear down on the defence, draw opponents to him or, if the situation was right, take the Wilkins route of the immediate pass. There is no Bobby Charlton around but there is Steve McMahon. McMahon may lack the consistency of players of the highest class but he has much more to offer England than Wilkins. He does have a change of pace, he can win the ball and he can put defences under pressure by bursting forward.

Liverpool team-mate but international foe Ray Houghton has no doubts about the inspirational qualities of the fair-haired Mc-Mahon. In his book, Houghton, one of Jack Charlton's key players in the Republic of Ireland side, wrote: 'He is simply an out and out winner. He chases, he intimidates and he simply refuses to give up.' Glenn Hysen of Sweden and now Liverpool describes McMahon as a 'superman'. Hysen and McMahon have crossed swords on the international scene, and Hysen, rated one of the most gifted sweepers in the world game, says: 'He is one of the hardest men to play against. He offers so much to the attack and also helps cover the defence. The last player we wanted to face in our World Cup qualifying game in Stockholm was ... Steve McMahon.'

McMahon was given his England chance by Robson in Israel in February 1988. He travelled to Tel Aviv expecting to be nothing more than a substitute. Bryan Robson's hamstring strain in training pushed McMahon into a satisfactory debut. There was enough promise to keep him in the squad. But the more he played for England in those early days, the more complex it became. He lost his way with England. Then, he deputized for England's Captain Fantastic in Sweden. His performance was of the highest calibre, and he proved he was the man to take over from the injured Neil Webb for the World Cup. Jimmy Hill observed at the time:

> The heroic blood-stained performance of Terry Butcher and two flashes of genius from Peter Shilton in Stockholm almost obscured Steve McMahon, who produced the best midfield show I have seen for many a year. He took the game by the scruff of the neck from the outset, was hungry for the ball and tackled in his usual aggressive fashion. But, more than that, he sprayed a stream of varied, accurate passes which oiled the wheels in midfield and brought fluency to an area where it has been missing. Having looked at a tape of the game again, he didn't give away possession once, and the timing of his passes was so beneficial. Players who give you the ball early and at the right weight are a blessing — and Steve was just that. There is a moment when an outstanding League player turns into something more than that and it happened for McMahon in this game. He received a good press after the friendly against Israel, which really meant nothing. The pitch was a joke and no one could fairly be judged in those circumstances. But this was different — a new international was born.

McMahon has shown the world he can fill the boots of Graeme Souness and Bryan Robson. But for the brilliance of the Manchester United and England skipper, McMahon would have won far more caps. It is a parallel situation to that of Norman Hunter who acted as Bobby Moore's understudy between 1966 and 1974, with Hunter winning 24 of his 28 caps in that period, while Moore made 77 of his 108 appearances for England.

I first realized there was a side to Steve McMahon that the public had no notion about when I interviewed him just a few days after the Hillsborough tragedy. The interview was taken from the *Daily Mirror* sports pages by the editor of the day, Richard Stott, and used as a centre-page spread. Steve McMahon's sentiments at that time should never be forgotten, and I feel it is appropriate to reproduce the article in its entirety:

Steve McMahon is the hard man of the Liverpool team, the player whose bone-shaking tackles are a legend at Anfield.

Yesterday, the hard man wept. Wept unashamedly in front of his wife and two small sons as he opened his heart to me about the horror of Hillsborough and the agony of its aftermath.

'I do believe in God . . .' he told me. 'But if God does exist how could he let this happen?

'"Daddy, why were those people crushed?" one of my boys asked me. I don't know what to tell him.

'I've wept for those dead. There have been so many tears, and there will be more.'

Steve was born and bred on Merseyside. Some of the victims are his friends and neighbours.

Indeed, the first news he had of the tragedy was brought to him on the field at Hillsborough by two fans he knew.

'Two lads leapt over the fences and were running on the pitch. I was shocked because I recognized their faces. They live in the same area as me!

'They ran straight over to me. They told me their friends were back there getting crushed.

'I didn't realize what was going on . . . I thought it was a pitch invasion.'

Steve's voice tails off. He stares at the floor, lost in his own thoughts . . .

Minutes seem to pass. Then he is talking again, telling me of two visits he has made that he knows will live with him for ever.

One was to deserted Anfield, to the shrine to the dead in the goal in front of The Kop. The other was to the two Sheffield hospitals where many of the victims still lie.

'One of the first people I saw in hospital was a man lying in his bed with his wife [sitting] beside him.

'He had just come out of intensive care. His life had been spared. Yet he was so depressed.

'He told me that he didn't care about himself. He had lost his 14-year-old boy.

'In the crush his son slipped away from him, he couldn't get near him to save him.

'He didn't blame the police. He didn't blame anyone. He just kept saying, "I blame myself, I should have saved him".

'It really brought everything home to me. I've got two boys of my own.

'We gave him a Liverpool shirt. He said that his lad would have loved that, he would have given it to him.

'Then he said: "I'll bury him in that shirt."'

The tears well again. Then Steve goes on: 'I also saw two lads in intensive care.

'Both were in coma, but they came to when they heard our voices.

'Do you know what the first words of one of them were? "How did Everton get on?" Incredible.

'When the other boy came to and saw us he started shouting the names of the team.

'He knew who was who and somehow we felt as though we knew him.

'The medical staff were amazed. One minute victims were on life-support machines, the next they were sitting up and talking to us.

'Another, in the middle bed, was a lad called Andy Gregory. His girlfriend spotted me and came rushing over.

'"He idolizes you, Steve, please go up and speak to him. Try to wake him up, there isn't much hope, but try."

'It was the least I could do . . . but he didn't wake up.

'The doctors told me that he showed some signs of response, but just a little. They explained that although he is asleep he can hear you.

'It is hard to talk to somebody who can't talk back to you. But I didn't worry. I kept on talking. I was just sad that I couldn't do more.

'His girlfriend was so grateful.

'Then she asked me: "Can you kiss him?" So I kissed him.'

The Liverpool players were at the hospital for four hours and must have spoken to at least forty people.

'We spent as much time as we could chatting to people,' Steve says.

That hospital visit on Monday did more for the footballer than he dreamt was possible.

'I felt so much better knowing I had done something positive to help,' he says simply.

'I was distraught on Sunday night after the Liverpool Cathedral service. The enormity of what had happened didn't hit me on Saturday as I sat in a silent dressing-room.

'But in the Cathedral it all came home to me.

'When I came out I have never felt so low, so frustrated, so helpless.

'I knew I wanted to go back to the ground. Supporters had been going there all day. I wanted to go.'

Steve joined Roy Evans, one of the 'boot-room boys'. Together they made their own private pilgrimage to the spiritual home of the Liverpool terrace supporters, The Kop.

'When we got there it must have been 7 p.m. The gates were locked but we got in through a side gate. There were still thousands of fans outside wanting to come in.

'The place was deserted apart from Roy and myself. I walked up to the goal-mouth.

'I was stunned by what I saw ... messages, tributes, flowers, scarves. Not just red scarves of Liverpool, but the blue of Everton.

'It was so sad. Yet at the same time it was everything that Merseyside people are all about. Fantastic people!

'One message will always stick with me. "Down here at Anfield you will be sadly missed. Don't worry, Bill Shankly will be waiting for you up there."

'I still believe in God. That was something to cling to.'

People began to look upon Steve McMahon in a different light after that article was published. Many people on Merseyside thanked him for expressing his innermost thoughts. It made many people feel that the players really cared for them, and for their plight.

Steve's attractive young wife Julie noticed a big change in her husband after Hillsborough.

'He grew up,' she says. 'He has a lot more time for people; he is more sensitive. Like most footballers, he took so much for granted, everything for granted. But no more.

'We both appreciate our sons Stephen and Paul even more than we used to. Steve recognizes how short life can be.'

Trevor Hicks, Chairman of the Hillsborough Family Support Group, lost his two daughters on the Leppings Lane terraces. He says:

> Steve was always Vicki's favourite player. Her most prized possession was a photo of Steve outside the team hotel before the FA Cup Final. Steve was her absolute hero and she often wrote about him. I didn't really know until after Hillsborough exactly what Vicki was up to in her scrap-book. She had taught herself to touch-type at the age of twelve and compiled match reports and players' profiles, obviously very biased reports!

Trevor sent photographs, 'match reports' and Steve's player profile to Steve McMahon when he discovered that he was compiling his autobiography.

Harry Harris,
Croydon, August 1990

Chapter 1

Family

MY FATHER THOMAS, now 47, has always been an Evertonian through and through. I was reared as a typical Evertonian, with blue blood in my veins. Under such circumstances it is quite unusual that I've turned out to be a Liverpool player. As soon as I was old enough, my dad took me to Goodison Park. I was around eight or nine when I attended my first soccer match there.

As for kicking a ball, I can't remember the time that I wasn't booting a ball around, and my dad was always encouraging me. In fact, he became my fiercest critic in my formative years as a player, as he was never satisfied with my performances. He no longer criticizes, that role has been taken over by my wife Julie. I affectionately call her Bobby, after former England manager Bobby Robson, for her critical appraisal of my performances for both club and country.

In fairness to my dad, he was doing the right thing. As a kid you don't really want people telling you how good you are, or you will never improve. You need someone able to spot your faults and try to correct them. For that I shall be eternally grateful to him.

At the age of seven or eight, football had virtually taken over my life. I just loved the game, and always wanted to be a professional footballer. I couldn't think of anything else I wanted to be, and I didn't want to be anything else. It's marvellous to have such uncomplicated and direct ambitions. It's even more gratifying to have fulfilled many of them.

My dad played for Liverpool Schoolboys, turned out at Anfield and even scored the winning goal at the Anfield Road end. When I broke into professional football and made my mark with Everton I said to him: 'I've done something you never managed, I've scored at Anfield's Kop end, as well as the Anfield Road end.' During the time I played for Everton there seemed no likelihood of scoring at any end at Anfield because we were battered in every Merseyside derby game! So, I was quite proud of my achievement of actually getting a couple of goals at Anfield.

My dad was courting since he was about twelve, and married my mum Irene at the age of 16. I've got three brothers and one sister, Maria. Thomas is the eldest brother, I'm next, then John and Christopher.

John, who is 26, is a very good footballer and was in fact a professional at Everton and I actually played in one reserve game under him as my captain! I was a first-team regular at the time, but I had been injured and was making my come-back in the reserves.

A nasty back injury badly affected John's footballing career. He cracked a bone at the base of his spine and needed surgery to repair it. Perhaps another problem for him was the fact that I left Everton in less than amicable circumstances when my contract expired, and I walked out to join Aston Villa. I felt the contract offered to me to stay at Goodison wasn't good enough, and it may well have been that my departure didn't do John any favours, although I couldn't say for sure whether the club took it out on him. Yet, I couldn't help but feel guilty when his career came to an end at Everton; I felt responsible because he was not really given a chance. He was captain of the reserves when he received a letter from Colin Harvey informing him that he would not be retained.

I got John a trial at Aston Villa shortly after I signed for the Midlands club. He stayed with me for two weeks, and I thought that they liked his game. Then, again, they may well have given John that trial out of courtesy to me. Whatever the reasons for taking him on for a fortnight, they eventually said that they had too many players at Villa Park and they couldn't offer him a contract. He was then scraping around seeking employment with a club. He tried Northampton but didn't like it. He now plays non-League football with Altrincham, and he is an assistant manager at the Halewood Sports Complex.

Thomas works in Fords factory, while Chris has a spell in London as a security guard, and my sister Maria is a sewing-machinist. My dad is unemployed, but used to be a scaffolder — if he can remember that far back!

My father-in-law Peter has been a season-ticket holder at Anfield long before I ever played for them. When I returned home after signing for Liverpool, Peter said: 'That's the best thing that's ever happened to me.' Julie's mother, Lil, wasn't too keen on that remark, and replied: 'What about marrying me, then?' Peter thought about it for a while and stuck to his guns: 'No, Steve signing for Liverpool is still the best thing that has happened to me!'

You can imagine that he wasn't very popular with his missus for a little while after that episode.

In all seriousness, my family is very precious to me, especially my children. I adore my two boys, Stephen and Paul, and my wife Julie. I consider myself a family man: my family comes first, my football second.

Julie underwent a Caesarean for the birth of our first boy, Stephen, and she suffered a major operation, another Caesarean, for the premature arrival of little Paul. Not only was Paul premature, he was not quite right, there was a complication, and he spent the first three weeks fighting for his life in an incubator.

I signed for Liverpool in September with Julie already pregnant. Paul was born in December and because he was on a life-support machine, the club told me to take as much time off as possible. But it was an awful time. I would train in the morning and then rush off to the hospital and spend the rest of the day at Paul's side.

Julie's mum was marvellous, she was always there when she was needed, and so too was her dad Peter.

I was so afraid because it was touch and go, and the doctors were so worried about Julie that they told me the full extent of Paul's problems but advised me against telling Julie. Naturally, I confided in my mum and dad, and they advised me to consult a priest to read the last rites just in case the worst happened. I declined. I simply felt that to bring in a priest was tempting fate. I just refused to accept that it could happen, and I had faith that it wouldn't, blind faith perhaps.

It's not for me to say, but I've heard it said about me that I'm fearless on the pitch, that I would not back out of any tackle. Well, this was the time I was frightened, frightened for the life of my baby. Paul was eight weeks premature, he wasn't properly formed, he couldn't breathe properly, and lumps had formed all over his body. The doctors told me that he was 'critical'.

A baby was born at the same time as Paul, premature, with the same condition as Paul's. That baby didn't make it; when we returned to the hospital a few weeks later we discovered that he had died.

Paul's condition lasted the best part of a month and through it all I played on for Liverpool. In my first season for Liverpool, the club won the coveted League Championship and FA Cup Double, but there was something far more important, far more precious to me, and that was the well-being of little Paul.

No one knew or could even begin to imagine the sort of thoughts running through my mind even when I was diving in to make tackles on opponents. During the first match, I was in a total state of shock. Concentration is the hallmark of any good professional, but on that day I didn't have a clue what was going on around me.

I was playing like a machine, from memory, the entire game was a blur. I'd be lying if I said I was thinking about football. I wasn't. In fact, I didn't really care about the match. For the first time in my life I came to realize that football was only a game, it didn't really matter if we won or lost, or whether I played badly or not, yet despite all this I played and it wasn't the least bit important to me. The one thing that was important to me, more than anything in the world, was away from me and my wife in an incubator on a life-support machine, and there were all sorts of dark thoughts at the back of my mind.

It's an old saying that it never rains but it pours, and when things are at their lowest there are even other problems. Because of the transfer we didn't have a home of our own at this time. When I first moved to Liverpool, we first tried a hotel, then moved out to my mum and dad's, and eventually a friend put us up. Paul Lodge and his wife turned out to be real friends, true friends, friends who were all too ready to help out when we really needed them most. Paul used to play for Everton; in fact, he played some thirty odd games before switching to non-League after spells with Bolton and Preston. When Julie's pregnancy became a major problem, Paul and his missus moved out of their own home to help us out and they moved to Paul's mum's place! That is a real pal.

Paul finally came out of hospital on Christmas Eve – that was the best Christmas present of all time. We decided that we would declare with two kids, there would be no more problem births for Julie.

For the rest of my life I shall be eternally grateful to the nurses, doctors and staff at the Oxford Street Maternity Hospital in Liverpool. Whenever I'm asked to nominate my favourite charity, it gives me such enormous pleasure to select the special care maternity unit. I've sent them autographed shirts to raise money in auctions.

Chapter 2

Ball-boy

WHEN I FIRST SIGNED schoolboy forms for Everton I was paid 50p a time as a ball-boy at Goodison Park for home games. It was a way of letting a promising youngster get a taste of the big match atmosphere, almost as part of the action. I'm sure it worked in my case. Sitting there watching my heroes play from such close range certainly spurred me on even more to wanting desperately to become a professional footballer. I would report before the game and sit with the pressmen, until it was time to change in a room near to the players' dressing-rooms.

I would take my little stool and sit behind the goal in my green track-suit top. It was a smashing day out for me because I was an Everton supporter as well, so I got into the games for free. I've seen that picture of me as an Everton ball-boy looking tense during the game; well, I'm not surprised – I was biting my nails and worried because in those days Everton didn't win too many games!

Out of that 50p fee I would have to pay my bus fares, and I needed to take two buses from home to the ground. On the way home I'd stop with my mate Brian Burrows, who was also one of the ball-boys, and buy a bag of chips for six pence. If we could afford it, we would share a piece of fish.

There were some games, when Everton played Newcastle or Sunderland in particular, when it became quite a hazard being a ball-boy. The fans would hurl coins on to the pitch and there were times when I was struck on the back of the head. Actually, I didn't mind, and nor did my mates. It didn't really hurt and I wanted them to throw more! I would spend most of the match collecting the coins – and that definitely meant a fish supper on the way home. When the crowd got really angry I could collect a few pounds! I suppose you could say that was my tip.

Some ball-boys keep the ball too long and waste time when their club is hanging on for a result; some ball-boys throw the ball back into play too quickly. I was never guilty of either of those tricks, but we did have our little scam at Goodison when we were ball-boys for reserve games. We would bring a ball along and play a game under the stand where no one could see us. We would post a look-out who would retrieve the ball when necessary. The game would start with five or six ball-boys in the stand, but during the match there only seemed to be *one* in action. He was the volunteer who would keep popping his head up to see if the ball was coming our way. Anything that resembled two posts became the goals. We enjoyed our games, and never got caught.

I was a ball-boy for two years. My brothers John and Christopher were also ball-boys at Everton, all three of us at the same time. We were once interviewed on Granada TV when I had got into the first team. When we were asked about our footballing aspirations I replied: 'Yes, I have always wanted to be a footballer and play for Everton.' Next, it was John's turn. 'Yes, I have always wanted to play professional football for Everton.' Then, it came to Christopher. 'I want to be a fruit and veg. man. I don't like football all that much!'

There is no doubt that being a ball-boy is an exhilarating

experience and gives you a terrific feel for the atmosphere of a big First Division game.

I was a ball-boy when Bob Latchford became the first to score 30 goals in a season, collecting the ball from the back of the net when he notched his thirtieth. There had been a lot of hype about it and he received a big cheque for doing it. I sat on my stool watching him complete a superb hat-trick from the penalty spot, and then retrieved the ball. A few years later I played in the same Everton team as Latchford! He scored twice when I played with him in a match at Blackpool. One day I was picking the ball out of the net for him as a ball-boy, the next I was jumping on his shoulders helping him to celebrate one more of his many goals for Everton.

But it was not a smooth passage to the top. Football is littered with hard-luck experiences of players who have drifted out of the game but might have, one day, become exceptional talents. I could have been one of them. Everton didn't think I would make the grade as a professional footballer. They told me I was too weak and small. Perhaps I had the ability, but not the physique. I was 15 years old and advised to get on my bike and find myself a job.

I signed on the dole and collected £16 a week, but it never crossed my mind to find employment because I only knew one thing and that was football. I was among a group of apprentices due to be taken on as professionals at that time, but I wasn't. Yet, I was determined to make it, and Everton gave me just a little hope – they said they would pay my bus fare to continue to train at the club! I would sign on the dole in the morning, collect my pay, and then sprint to catch the bus to get to training by 10.30 a.m.

Brian Burrows, who went on to play for Coventry, was in the same situation – a reject, but refusing to give up. We both carried on as amateurs, and it was a hard existence. We would both sign on the dole together, catch the bus together, share our sandwiches, and even wear identical duffle coats we bought from the Army and Navy store to try to protect us from the cold. It cost us a week's dole money to pay for those coats. But we needed them because the bus was a mile away from the dole office. Everton provided us with expenses of £4 a week for our bus fares.

Thankfully, Colin Harvey was the reserve team coach and he had faith in me. He gave me the best piece of advice in my entire football career. He told me to do some weight training during the summer break to build myself up. I sweated blood, working out four days a week, but it is nice to look back and know it was all worth the effort. I was pumping iron for a month and when I returned to the club for pre-season they couldn't recognize me! I'd put on a stone in weight. I was no longer being brushed off the ball, or lasting only an hour in the game. I trained with the club until I was eighteen when they finally signed me as a professional.

I wonder what I would have done had I failed to make it. I'm an outdoors type, I just couldn't imagine myself in a factory, I'd go mad. I would have had to find some job in the fresh air. I would not have pursued any other professional sport; I was never anywhere near special at anything else.

In fact, academically I was a wash-out at school, until the third form when I realized that education was important, but even so my mind was always on the moment the bell would signal the end of school and I could concentrate on playing football. But the teachers always had a powerful weapon in persuading me to switch my attention to school work – they threatened me with a ban from school matches unless I improved academically. Of course, nothing was going to keep me from football, so I became a good scholar! At least, as good as I could be.

I attended St Andrew's High School in Halewood, and I've kept the letter from the Headmaster when I left school in June 1977.

> To Whom It May Concern, Stephen McMahon has attended this school since 5 September 1972. He is always polite, clean and dresses tidily.
>
> Stephen has followed a five-year course at this school leading to the CSE in which he took the following subjects: Art, English, German, History, and Maths; also GCE History, Geography, Art and Government, Economics and Commerce. The results are not yet to hand.
>
> On the physical side he has taken a full part in the gymnastic and athletic activities of the school programme and has accredited himself well.
>
> As a senior pupil he was selected for School Prefect, a task which, in a rapidly growing school, is no easy matter, carrying as it does a certain responsibility for supervision and safety of younger boys moving about the school.
>
> In conclusion we would like to wish him every success in whatever sphere he may choose for his future career.

In his own handwriting the Headmaster added a PS: 'Stephen has played in Liverpool City Schoolboy Teams both juniors and senior since he was 11 years old and is an excellent athlete.'

In my early days as a player, around the age of thirteen, I was a centre-forward playing for Vernon Colts in a local league. We were the top team; no one could match us in our age group. We were unbeaten for four years.

In one particular game, we were winning 12, no, it may have been 13–0 at half-time, and I scored 10 of them. The whistle blows for half-time and our team manager takes me off! I'm substituted after scoring 10 goals in the first half. Not surprisingly, I couldn't believe it. He must have placed a bet on the other team. You would have thought he would have wanted me to carry on scoring as many as I could.

The first contract I signed for Everton was dated 19 December 1977, and it was countersigned by club secretary Jim Greenwood. The terms were £16 a week from the date I signed it until 20 August 1978, and then £20 a week until 20 August 1979. The win bonuses were written into the agreement, and were £2 in a reserve match, £1 for an 'A' or 'B' game or any other youth match, and for the FA Youth Cup there was a £1 bonus for getting to Round Two, £1.50 to reach Round Three, £2.50 Round Four, £3.50 Round Five, £4 for a Semi-Final place, and £6 for the Final.

What a difference from my current six-year contract with Liverpool! I'm not going into detail about my contract, because I believe that a player's salary should be confidential while they are still under the terms of that deal. Also, it can lead to internal problems with other players who might feel upset if they are not on similar wages. Equally, I might feel aggrieved if I discovered a certain player on higher wages than myself.

Certainly, Liverpool players are on excellent wages, among the top-paid players in British football, with big bonuses geared to success. But there are only a handful of clubs in the country capable of paying those sort of salaries — Liverpool, Everton, Manchester United, Spurs and Arsenal — the so-called Big Five. People have got the wrong impression because the majority of professional foot-ballers are not earning the sort of lavish sums the general public are led to believe. There are also thousands of youngsters who fail to make the grade, dreaming of making a million and ending up as hardship cases. That's the down side, but there is always the chance of making the grade in a big way, if you have the talent and the determination. The rewards are there for the star players.

I would recommend professional football to an aspiring youngster, but that may be because of my experiences and that it has worked out well for me. Whereas if you sought the opinion and advice of someone who had failed to make it, they might have a vastly different outlook. Yet, my brother desperately wanted to reach the top as a professional footballer, and he had talent, yet he didn't make it. That did sour me somewhat, but overall I still believe professional football is a vocation worth pursuing. I would not push my boys into the game, but I would give them every encouragement if they showed the willingness, temperament, and the talent.

But I have always maintained that a footballer's life is a short one, and a player's maximum earning potential is even shorter. I'm sure the public don't take that into consideration when they see players earning thousands a week. I feel I have more than adequately demonstrated my loyalty to Liverpool by signing such a long-term contract when I could have waited until my contract had expired and then walked out to go abroad, with clubs like Sampdoria hovering in the background.

I signed the six-year term as security for my family. Players can be cut down overnight through injury. It is a hazard that claims many players each season and causes much grief and heartache.

I suffered my first serious injury in my first season of senior football with Everton. Fortunately, there were only half a dozen or so games left at the end of that season when I played at West Brom. I played the ball back to my goalkeeper when, from the side, Remi Moses came in and went right through me. Whether he meant to go for the ball, or not, I shall never know. But he took me and the ball at the same time – most unlike him! I was in quite a bit of pain.

I got to my feet, but as soon as I put my foot down, the knee gave way. The trainer came on, but it was clear that it was something serious. In fact, I had snapped the medial ligament; it was completely severed, and I was carted off to hospital immediately for surgery. It required a very tricky operation that kept me out for the rest of that season and it was a struggle to get myself fit for the start of the following season. I was in hospital for ten days; it was a major operation, and whether I played again was a case of 'wait-and-see'.

As a young lad, it was a very frightening experience. The true significance of my situation didn't really sink in. When I left hospital, in plaster from the bottom of my leg to the top, I began to wonder whether I would ever play again. I had a few nightmares, but I just couldn't accept that my career might be finished before it had really even started.

The road back to full fitness was a punishing one. With my leg in plaster for nearly two weeks the muscles had 'wasted', and I couldn't bend the knee. The real hardship was to gain full mobility in my knee, and at one stage the specialist recommended that I fall down the stairs – by accident on purpose! He said that would be 'ideal', but I never really had the courage to go through with it. The specialist felt such a traumatic movement would be the only method to make the complete breakthrough, to extend the knee fully, but I preferred to let nature take its course, and that was certainly hard work right the way through the summer months.

I missed a fabulous end-of-season tour to the Far East, and all I managed was one week's holiday in Florida, where the swimming helped. When I returned I did a lot more swimming to build up the thigh muscle back to its normal size, to protect the knee before I could start running and then jogging.

I started the next season in the reserves at Bolton, even though I had made a complete recovery and felt I was fit enough. Howard Kendall was the manager and he did things his way. Even though the first team won 3–1 on the opening day of the season at home to Birmingham City, he brought me back into the team for the mid-week match with Leeds!

Three years later, I was with Aston Villa, and it was Remi Moses' turn to go off injured after a tackle by me, but there were certainly no malice or revenge motives involved. Moses' career was prematurely ended, with the first of his many injury problems traced back to my tackle. But it was a legitimate tackle with the ball there to be won, and the two of us went in, as both Remi Moses and I would go for the ball, with total commitment and determination to win possession, not to cripple the opponent. Unfortunately, he had to go off, and I took no satisfaction in such a terrible sight for any player. In fact, the referee didn't even award a foul against me for that tackle because there was no way it was a dodgy challenge. It is ironic that it had been me last time, but these things happen.

But it fills me with great sadness that he should have been lost to the game, particularly as he was on the fringe of the England squad. I wouldn't want to see any player go out of the game and it was such a shame for Remi who was at the peak of his career.

The second major operation occurred in September 1988, this time with Liverpool, and once again it put my career on the line. I had a hamstring injury with the tendon behind the knee damaged. On this occasion it was my own fault, in a game against Manchester United. Mike Duxbury had the ball and I stretched to make a block tackle. My leg was in the air and he caught it. At first I thought I had pulled the hamstring muscle, but over the weekend a stabbing pain at the back of the right knee developed. I saw the physio on Monday and straight away I was off to hospital for surgery.

Once again all the self-doubts began creeping into the back of my mind. How long would I be out? Would there be a bad reaction? Would I ever play again? The previous experience of major surgery certainly helped, as did my extra experience in the game, and also the specialist was absolutely superb. He reassured me, told me there were no complications after surgery and that he felt I would make a complete recovery. He just warned me not to rush back and to take every precaution.

I was in hospital for four days, in plaster for almost two weeks, and then it took two-and-a-half months' rehabilitation before I was back playing again. But after being included in the European Championship squad, this was a bad time to be missing for both club and country. It ruled me out for the international with Denmark and the World Cup qualifying game with Sweden in Stockholm. I'm the world's worst watcher, so this was the most frustrating period of my entire career.

Whenever I'm injured, whether it's a serious operation and I'm out of the game for a long period, or just a routine kick or strain that forces me to miss a single game, I'm not worth living with at home. I put Julie through hell. I'm always grumpy. It's far worse when I'm in plaster because I feel so helpless, and Julie tries to do so much to help, but all the pampering makes me feel worse.

Thankfully, I've been relatively lucky and steered clear of injury. My record positively confirms that I have not missed too many games. I have played well over 400 First Division matches. Perhaps I am a quick healer. I seem to be able to recover faster than most from knocks and scrapes.

More players are seeking private insurance cover to guard against the loss of their career through injury. Clubs take out insurance cover but the club would therefore benefit, rather than the player. It would then be at the discretion of the club to give the player a cash payment or a benefit match. Perhaps I have some old-fashioned ideas but I'm loathe to insure myself – I don't like tempting fate. Yet, that is a position I might review. After all, I do have life insurance, although the reason for that is to make sure the wife and kids would be well looked after if the worst came to the worst.

Incidentally, Liverpool have only recently employed a physiotherapist. When I signed for the club, Bob Paisley took me to Walton Hospital, about two or three minutes from the ground, and I was examined as a normal out-patient. I had to wait my turn and a doctor checked me out. It all took about ten minutes and I was back out again in the car, and away. The medical was very basic. It was as simple as making sure I could walk and I was OK to play for Liverpool.

It all changed at Anfield when Kenny Dalglish took over as manager. Before the new regime, the physio turned up for two hours between one and three, and the system was very simple: if a player had a knock or a bruise he would have treatment and then train. If the player failed to train leading up to a match, he wasn't fit to play. If the injury was serious the player would be sent to see the best specialist and surgeon. Examine the records over the years and Liverpool had precious few major injuries. The reason was quite simple: if you missed a game it was such a damn hard job to win back your place. It was best not to be injured and to be able to continue playing.

The attitude of some players is to avoid training all week, indulge in plenty of physiotherapy, yet miraculously report fit by Friday. It was different at Anfield. The management did not believe in malingering, and they certainly would not indulge in mollycoddling anyone, nor would they allow players to mope around 'thinking' they were injured. Bob Paisley had a knack with injuries; he could diagnose quite a lot of problems. He would argue that the treatment of injuries was really common sense most of the time. Roy Evans took a course in physiotherapy and also first aid, to act fast in case of head injuries or a player swallowing his tongue. But other clubs considered it important to have a full-time physio, and clearly Kenny thought it was time to have someone on a more regular basis and appointed Paul Chadwick part-time.

Roy Evans is the man who runs onto the pitch. He usually says: 'Where does it hurt?' Then he applies the wet sponge, the 'magic sponge'. He's got all the modern equipment and medication in his bag, but it must be for show. It seems to me he never uses anything but the wet sponge!

At Liverpool a player is frightened to go down injured in case they carry you off or put your number up, and put on the substitute.

Chapter 3

Captain of Everton and Liverpool

THE PROUDEST MOMENT of my life, the most fantastic honour of my footballing career, was to captain Liverpool. It was also a very significant occasion. It was on Saturday 28 April, 1990, in the decisive First Division match with Queens Park Rangers. I knew straight away, when the armband was thrown in my direction, that I was the first to skipper both Merseyside clubs. People tend to forget that I skippered Everton. I'm told that The Kop warmly applauded the decision that I should take over from the injured Alan Hansen, but I didn't notice it at the time. I was so proud, it lifted me another six inches.

The biggest problem was trying to get the damn armband on! Before the game the captain pins on the armband carefully, but it is tricky to secure it during the game with your attention elsewhere. I wouldn't have been very popular if I had concentrated on securing the armband and QPR had scored. Ronnie Moran shouted from the bench, 'Just leave it.'

Alan Hansen and Ronnie Whelan have captained Liverpool over the years since the departure of Graeme Souness. With quality players like them, and true leaders, I never thought the day would come that I would be skipper of such a great club.

Some might say I got the armband because I was the one closest to the touch-line, but I don't believe that! Although it was a privilege to take over as captain against QPR for the final twenty minutes or so, I wasn't sure it would go down officially as I was only stand-in skipper with Alan Hansen forced off injured. If there was any chance that it would have counted then I'd have claimed it! But for me, it was not the real thing, even though it was still a big thrill, particularly as the result came through that Aston Villa had only drawn with Norwich and the Championship was ours. My first experience of being truly in charge turned out to be such a magnificent occasion, the night we clinched the title – what an incredible feeling!

Four days after the QPR game, with Alan still out injured, I was captain of Liverpool leading the team out at Anfield against Derby County on the night the Championship and the Barclays trophy was presented to the club. Now, that is some honour in my book! And it certainly dispelled any notion that they threw the armband to me because I was the nearest!

There are not many in the history of the game who have played for both Merseyside clubs, let alone skipper the two, so I thought I might have become the first to do so. Add to that, the fact that I was the only Scouser to have won the Double, and I can't help feeling very proud. When Liverpool won the Double in my first season at the club, Gary Ablett, the only other Scouser, won a FA Cup winner's medal, but not a League Championship medal.

When I started out in the game I never dreamed that I would achieve so much. It just shows you what can be done. I considered it a marvellous achievement to captain Everton, then I moved on to Aston Villa, and when I signed for Liverpool I never imagined that one day I would lead out the team as captain.

I turned down Manchester United to join Liverpool, that's how much I wanted to sign for the club. Villa were playing at Southampton. Manager Tony Barton named the team at midday, then pulled me to one side to explain why I wasn't playing that night. It was the last few matches of the season and I was leaving. I had made it clear that I wanted to move back to the north. The manager said: 'I think you might like this move.' He informed me that Manchester United manager Ron Atkinson had made a satisfactory offer that had been accepted by Villa. I believe it involved a swop deal with Alan Brazil. I think I shocked Tony Barton when I replied: 'Thanks, but no thanks.' There had been a great deal of press speculation that Liverpool would move in, and I was prepared to bide my time for that chance. When the opportunity arose to sign for Liverpool I took it and it was the best decision of my career.

In five years at Anfield, last season was the first I had never been to a Wembley Cup Final; I had been part of the Double winning side in my first season, the next season it was the Littlewoods Cup, and then the FA Cup Final in successive seasons. The FA Cup Semi-Final defeat by Crystal Palace blew apart my record of going to Wembley for a fifth year in a row, and a hat-trick of FA Cup Finals. It also crushed my chance of another Double success. It was a funny experience going to Wembley for the 1990 FA Cup Final as a guest of a friend, watching the match in a big executive box together with Peter Beardsley. It wasn't the best-quality football I'd ever seen but there was plenty of excitement with Palace and United sharing six goals.

The Championship returned to Anfield and that partially made amends for our shock defeat in the Semi-Final by Palace and for losing in the title decider against Arsenal in the last game of the previous season. It showed a lot of character by everyone in the club to come back from that defeat by Arsenal. It was a shattering blow, inflicting terrible damage to morale within the club. I know we were severely criticized for adopting the wrong tactics in that final match of the season, shown in front of a live TV audience of ten million, that we were too cautious trying to play out a draw, knowing Arsenal had to win by two goals.

I feel that the season caught up on us after Hillsborough. I'm not making Hillsborough an excuse, that is the last thing I would do. But the facts are that we had to play too many games in such a short space of time. Perhaps, winning the FA Cup for the people was more important than winning the title.

Really, Arsenal's victory at Anfield that night doesn't bear thinking about. I still cannot believe it even now. But that's history. We proved again that we are the best team in the land by reclaiming the title. We demonstrated that we have the best players when we put our minds to it. But there can be no question that the defeat by Crystal Palace gave us a huge kick up the backside. It made us realize that if we didn't get our act together we would win absolutely nothing. We came back magnificently three days later, winning at Charlton despite almost half a team out injured, and on-loan striker Ronnie Rosenthal scoring a superb hat-trick. In fact, the Israeli international could have scored five or six that night, but he got three great goals.

Kenny Dalglish doesn't often take his team to task; he doesn't need to. But our FA Cup Semi-Final defeat by Palace was one of those rare occasions when he did need to. He was very, very disappointed when he came back into our dressing-room at Villa Park. He didn't say anything until he had had time to cool off in the showers. Then he called our performance 'unprofessional', and he was absolutely right. The amount of internationals in our team, with such a vast number of First Division games behind them, against a relatively inexperienced side like Palace, yet we threw away the Semi-Final. All credit to Palace for working hard at their set pieces, but they took advantage of our mistakes and Kenny wasn't going to tolerate that. To think we had slaughtered them 9–0 in the League at Anfield and won 2–0 at Selhurst Park, an aggregate of 11–0 that season – and then to lose 4–3!

Everyone was upset at the time, and Ronnie Moran and Roy Evans had a few words to say. Kenny Dalglish and his back-room staff are strong-willed people, they don't need to go in for amateur dramatics, like some managers, slamming dressing-room doors and throwing cups and saucers around the place.

Immediately after the game, no one spoke for fifteen minutes. There was no point. Anything said then would have been all very heated and would have been regretted later, and only said in the heat of the moment anyway with probably nothing good coming from it. Everyone bit their lip, had a shower or a bath, and gave themselves time to put things into perspective.

Kenny Dalglish came out of the shower and started to dissect the game and said: 'Could we have done that or this?' He was particularly perturbed that we had given silly free kicks away from which Palace had profited. He went over to certain individuals to discuss their part in the defeat. He blamed me for the Palace equalizer. He said that I was responsible and asked: 'What was I thinking of?'

We kicked off the second half, the ball instantly coming back to me and I played a ball over the top aimed for John Barnes. Unfortunately, I misplaced the pass, it fell behind Barnes and was picked up by full-back John Pemperton. The right-back showed great pace as he went forward. I was dashing back to cover and I knew then I had made a terrible error and kept thinking, 'I've blown it'. I could smell the danger the moment I gave the ball away. In fact, I feared the worst. I got back to the goal-line by the time that Pemperton had crossed the ball and Mark Bright lashed into the roof of the net . . . off the top of my head.

That goal brought Palace into the game and gave them enormous confidence. It was perhaps the turning-point of the game; it was certainly one of the crucial points of the match. I blame myself for it, and for letting them back in the game. It made me feel sick, particularly as we had played some great stuff and they never looked like scoring or even having a chance.

The manager made it plain that he blamed me for that goal, too. Yes, he had a go at me. He said: 'You should not have over hit that pass, there was no need to have tried such a pass, it would have been easier to have just kept the ball.'

I scored the goal that seemed to have saved the Semi-Final, but Palace won in extra time. It was not a happy time for me, the team, or anyone at the club.

At my other clubs, Everton and Aston Villa, there were many Monday morning show-down meetings to thrash out the weekend defeats. That was not the case at Anfield. There were few bad defeats, for a start! But the general policy was not to hold weekly team meetings either to analyse defeats or crow about victories. The policy is to let you get on with it. But if there was a time that called for a team meeting, then we would have one. The only such team meeting of the season came after our Semi-Final defeat by Palace.

We reported at the ground before departing for the Tuesday night game against Charlton at Selhurst. On the pitch at Anfield, the manager called all the players round. He went through all the four Palace goals. It was not a question of apportioning blame any more, it was time to work out how to eradicate the deficiencies, to ensure that they didn't happen again.

I took the blame for the first goal, and the third was a total mix-up between our keeper Bruce Grobbelaar, Glen Hysen and young Steve Staunton. Steve tried to chest the ball down two yards away from his own goal-line, and he was honest enough to say, 'I could have headed it away.'

For the fourth goal, David Burrows said he could have headed the ball but thought it was going out of play. He had misjudged it as Andy Thorn flicked on the corner for Alan Pardew, three yards out, to head the winner. Kenny Dalglish made the point that from three yards out he should have been tightly marked.

We stuttered early in the season in our home games. We also lost 4–1 at Southampton but that was our once-every-season poor result to remind us that things don't come easily, that we cannot expect just to turn up and have everything our own way; we have to earn the right to play our football, and that means hard graft. At least, that's what we thought until our defeat against Palace.

But we had our high points. Beating Manchester United at Old Trafford was one of them. They boasted a proud record against us and always said how much they like playing us at Old Trafford. Our 3–1 triumph was not merely satisfying because of the margin of victory, but also because of the quality of our football.

But there can be no doubt that the defeat by Palace spurred us on to win the Championship. Yet, it annoys me intensely that our achievements have been undervalued by some people, mostly those only too ready to knock Liverpool. They have said it has been an average First Division, lacking in real quality, and this has been a poor Liverpool team in comparison to those in the past. Well, I just cannot accept any of that. We conceded the least number of goals in the First Division, we lost the least number of games, and won more than anyone else. Is that a poor team? I don't think so. We won the title by nine points – that's good enough for me. Everyone had been raving about how well Aston Villa had done, what a great season they'd had. Yet, they finished second, nine points behind us.

Chapter 4

Hillsborough

THE DAY BEGAN like any other big match for Liverpool. On this particular FA Cup Semi-Final day the sun shone brightly and all the players were anticipating an epic encounter with Nottingham Forest.

The pre-match build-up was precisely as it always was; it is clockwork with a club like Liverpool. With such a successful club, an FA Cup Semi-Final is almost routine. Our concentration was on the task ahead, the belief was there that we had the ability to reach the Final, we were all thinking that it would turn out to be a fabulous day for us all. Nothing even remotely entered our heads about how the day would eventually turn out.

2 p.m. Our coach arrived at Hillsborough after the normal preparation, and we all felt confident although naturally keyed up for such an important occasion. We strolled from our coach into the ground, to the dressing-rooms, and the players went through their usual routine.

2.10 My sister, Maria, travelled to the game with her boyfriend Peter. I gave them two terrace tickets for the Leppings Lane end. Peter's two brothers were also at the match and they had two seats in the stand. They swopped tickets so that my

sister and Peter could be in the stand, and Peter's two brothers
went on to the Leppings Lane terraces. I met them at the players'
entrance to sort out their tickets. There was no mention from
anyone I saw outside or inside the ground about any crowd
problems.

2.20 Once more, the normal practice for the Cup Semi-Final,
or indeed any match, is for the players to walk out on to the
pitch to test the playing-surface conditions, sample the atmosphere, and generally try to relax. When I look back now I
realize that there was something strange, almost eerie.

We all expected the ground to be around three-quarters full
for such a big game, even at this stage. Yet, it was weird,
because I remember thinking to myself that there weren't a lot of
people in the ground at this time. Julie was in the stands for a
long time because the wives had arrived so early with their
coach given a police escort, and she recalls that the ground
seemed surprisingly empty and then all of a sudden, shortly
before the kick-off, it was heaving.

2.30 The players were assembled in the changing rooms
waiting for our manager Kenny Dalglish to announce the team,
as it was the custom of the manager to keep even his players
guessing until this late hour for the final line-up. As it happened,
when Kenny announced the side there was a major surprise in his
selection. Alan Hansen, who had not played for several weeks,
was chosen out of the blue at centre-half. I have never seen Alan
Hansen looking so nervous before a game. He is normally so
cool, calm and collected, nothing ruffles him, but on this occasion
he seemed completely 'gone'.

3.05 It was a big match, a big atmosphere, a big crowd.
Everything as you'd expect. Normal. No news of any trouble
had filtered through to the players in the opening minutes of the
game. In fact, everything was fine from Liverpool's point of view

as we had the edge in the early exchanges, even though it was end to end stuff. We had won a corner and Peter Beardsley struck a shot that cannoned off the bar. Forest broke away into our half; I was running back towards our goal and was therefore looking towards our crowd behind the goal and I could see quite a few fans streaming on to the pitch.

My first thoughts were: 'Oh, my God, here we go again, supporters on the pitch spoiling it for everyone else.' That was the natural instinctive reaction because there had been so many examples of crowd disturbances and pitch invasions all over the country at various times. Julie, from her vantage-point in the stand, could see far more than I could, but the immediate feeling from the fans around her was that there was fighting going on, and there were one or two blokes around Julie shouting abuse at those fans when they began spilling on to the pitch.

3.06 The match was halted by a policeman running on to the pitch, although I didn't see him. But within seconds of spotting dozens of fans climbing over the high fences and pouring on to the pitch, I knew the truth. I was standing there on the pitch when a lad I knew from where I used to live in Halewood ran over to me and was clearly so distressed and agitated that I was sure straight away that something ghastly was going on. This lad was shouting at me in terrible fear, the fear was visible on his features; he shouted at me: 'There are people dying in that crush in there.' He pleaded with me to do something about it. I didn't know what to do. I didn't really know what was going on in there, or how I could help. I felt so helpless, there was nothing I could do.

The two sets of players were taken off the pitch straight away. In our dressing-rooms we didn't know if anyone was dead or injured, or what was really happening. We had no idea of the extent of the tragedy. Deep down I knew.

Yet, at this time, there was still a chance of the game going ahead, no matter how absurd that may sound, and we were all jogging on the spot, keeping our limbs warm, keeping loose as both teams thought that at any time we would be back on the pitch with the FA Cup Semi-Final resuming. We were not told until an hour later that the game had been officially, formally, finally called off. We knew what had happened.

3.36 Several fans filtered through to the dressing-room area, and there were a few desperately anxious to get into our changing rooms; they urgently wanted to, not only to inform the players what was going on, but to register their protests that there was a suggestion that the game would continue. Clearly, they remembered the indignity of Heysel when the European Cup Final went ahead.

They were upset and desperately wanted to let us know that the game *could not* go on after what had happened. A few were screaming: 'There are a couple of my mates dead out there, and you lot are still thinking of playing on.' I could hear another shout: 'If you play this match with our supporters lying dead it will be an absolute disgrace.' One lad, who was determined that the game must not carry on, actually got through the door to the dressing-room, but he was quickly ushered out by either Kenny Dalglish or Ronnie Moran.

By this time, there were a couple of supporters sitting on the floor outside our dressing-room crying their eyes out. Kenny Dalglish went outside to console them. But the manager wouldn't let us leave the sanctuary of our dressing-room. He issued strict instructions to that effect. You've got to remember that at this stage the game had not been officially called off, and the manager simply wanted to calm us down, in case we were told to play on. Kenny spoke to the supporters and found out precisely what had occurred.

4.00 The referee came into the dressing-rooms and officially informed us that the game had been called off, but we already knew that there was no chance of the match carrying on. The news had filtered through, all right. We had heard that there were ten people dead, then it was twenty, then thirty. It just went up and up in stages. Even if the FA wanted the game to go on, even if the referee had walked in and said play on, I don't think there was a single player in our dressing-room who had the stomach, who had the guts to walk back on to that football pitch to play a game of soccer. Half the players were in a state of shock, half had been slowly getting changed in any case.

There was precious little conversation in our dressing-room, which is usually alive with banter, but on this occasion no one had anything to say. John Barnes was in a terrible state. He couldn't say anything to anybody. He was inconsolable; he was in tears. Even Susie couldn't calm him down, she just put her arm around him in an effort to comfort him. The full impact of what had happened just seemed to hit Barnsie right away, yet it didn't really strike home to the rest of us until the next day or, maybe, in some cases, even a day or two later, perhaps because we were in such a state of shock. Julie was in shock, so were the rest of the wives, but John Barnes immediately felt part of the tragedy, while the rest of us began to worry about our family and friends.

The only mutterings I could pick up were the players' concern for family and friends who were at the game. My first thought was for my sister and her boyfriend, Peter's two brothers, and Julie's brother Paul who was standing on the Leppings Lane terraces. I felt so relieved that Maria had swopped tickets to sit in the stand rather than be in the Leppings Lane end, yet I was still so worried about her safety. I kept thinking that she could have been on the terracing.

All the players and their wives were anxiously waiting to use the one telephone outside the dressing-rooms. Fortunately, we were also given a portable phone. Julie and I were both panicking, because we had so many relatives and friends to check up on. It must have been 7 p.m. before we had checked that everyone had got home safely. Maria and Peter finally got home by bus. Peter's brothers had also survived, although they were not in the centre pen but on the left-hand side. Even so, they told us later of their experiences and their difficulties in getting on to the terraces.

Sunday   Every Sunday I visited my mum, and because I was there with Julie and the kids, Liverpool Football Club had trouble contacting me. Kenny's wife, Marina, was involved in rounding up all the players and their wives to attend a specially arranged Memorial Service at Liverpool Cathedral. By the time the club had got the message to me, there was no time to get home and change. I was stuck there in my track suit, so I dashed round to one of my mum's neighbours to borrow a suit. It nearly fitted, but I was grateful for the suit; I don't think it would have been a good idea to have turned up in a track suit for such an occasion. Because it was such short notice, Julie couldn't go and stayed with the kids.

The Memorial Service finally brought home to all the players the enormity of the tragedy. For those players who were shocked, stunned and busy worrying about relatives immediately after the match, they suddenly fully appreciated the extent of what had happened. Their emotions let loose. Bruce Grobbelaar gave a touching reading, and Kenny Dalglish also said a few words.

After the service, a coach took us back to Anfield. There were hundreds of people there. It was our first close contact with the fans since the tragedy, and now that became a full-time job; there was no training, no preparation for matches, no one thought about playing again – our thoughts were to help those in need of our help.

Monday 'The Gaffer' (Kenny Dalglish) called all the players to a team meeting and informed us that a coach had been arranged to transport us to Sheffield to visit those in hospital recovering from their injuries. It was a long, long journey to Sheffield, with the players keeping their thoughts very much to themselves. The players wanted to help but didn't know how to cope with such a situation. No matter what you say, you cannot put yourself into the shoes of all those people who were suffering so much. Some of us wondered, even feared, that we might get an angry reaction, that those people suffering emotionally would even resent our presence and tell us to get lost, that we didn't know what we were talking about. I wouldn't have blamed anyone for feeling that way, or reacting that way.

As it turned out, we visited three hospitals, and saw many of the survivors. We were welcomed by the injured; in fact, they were so glad to see us that the doctors and nurses told us that we had a therapeutic effect, and that made us feel really good, useful.

On one visit, the doctors turned the life-support machine off on a little boy. Alan Hansen got extremely upset, as did the rest of us.

The players and their wives became full-time social service workers, visiting the parents in their own homes of those who lost their lives, or meeting them at funerals. There were so many funerals every day, but we all felt honoured to be able to be present. Because of the amount of time involved, we split up our boys Stephen and Paul, with Paul staying with my mum and Stephen with Julie's mum. Kenny and Marina's family came down from Scotland to look after their children, and it was the same with all the players and their families.

From 9 a.m. to midnight we did as much as we could. Relatives, the survivors and the injured were welcomed into the players' lounge at Anfield to talk to the players and their wives, and we would offer as much comfort as humanly possible. The players' wives would humbly accept flowers from relatives of the bereaved to put on to the pitch, or hang scarves on the terraces.

I will never forget Eddie. He was sobbing in his hospital bed, on the day the players made one of their hospital visits. He had suffered terrible injuries to his ribs, arms, and shoulders but he lost his young son at the game, and kept blaming himself. His boy was crushed only inches from where he stood but it might as well have been a million miles away, with so many people tightly packed together he just couldn't reach him – and he blamed himself. Not the police, not the FA for the ticket allocation, he only blamed himself. That's when I knew there was nothing I could do for Eddie or for anyone else. But I tried. I told him that he was wrong to blame himself, because he wasn't to blame.

Blame! Yes, I blame the FA. I blamed them at the time and even now, long after Hillsborough, I blame the FA. I will never change my mind.

Liverpool's chief executive, Peter Robinson, complained to the FA about the club's ticket allocation long before the FA Cup Semi-Final, so I'm not being wise after the event. It was weeks beforehand that the club were deeply worried that Liverpool fans were not allocated The Kop end at Hillsborough. It just seemed common sense for the Liverpool fans to be accommodated in the larger area of terracing, considering the amount of supporters we have.

The FA's chief executive, Graham Kelly, was at the match and a lot of players delivered a few harsh words in his direction as we were coming off the pitch, myself included. I told him: 'Now you know why we should have had the other end of the ground.' There was a barrage of abuse from other players behind me, and most of them were spitting their venom towards Kelly in the general frustration of the situation.

But more than a year later I haven't changed my mind. Somebody must take responsibility, whether it is the police or the FA. They argued that it was more convenient to give the Forest fans The Kop end because it was easier access from the motorway, but a few diversions would have solved that problem.

As for the police, although I didn't know at the time what was happening, when the full facts emerged, it was clear just how many mistakes had been made by them. I still cannot understand why the police authorized the opening of the gate. It just seems to me they were shifting the problem from one area to make it far worse at another, but their attitude was simply to get rid of the problem they had where they had it. It was sickening to discover that the police had tried to blame the fans by saying that some were drunk and that they kicked open the gate.

I will always, for as long as I live, feel very badly about those who were to blame for so many unnecessary deaths.

Chapter 5

Post Hillsborough

MORE THAN A YEAR AFTER Hillsborough I'm still visiting the injured in hospital, regularly meeting relatives of the victims of the Leppings Lane terraces, and suffering the agonies of hearing about new heartaches relating to the tragedy. I know the rest of the country suffered along with Merseyside in the aftermath of Hillsborough, but I don't blame them for believing that we have mourned enough. And, so we have. We would all like to forget Hillsborough, but we cannot. Unfortunately for us, Hillsborough will never go away, it can never be forgotten, and there are so many reasons why it will not go away.

When the Liverpool team made their first hospital visit in Sheffield, I was asked to talk to a guy called Andy, who was in a coma. His family begged me to try to help him as I was always his favourite player. I spoke to him, held his hand, and just before I left him his girlfriend asked me to kiss him – which I did. I still visit Big Andy, he's 6ft. 3in., whenever I can, to this very day. He is out of coma, but it took so long that his brain was deprived of oxygen. He is still in hospital with brain damage and he will never recover; there is nothing to him, he can hardly communicate.

There are one, possibly two, fans still in hospital continuing to suffer from the aftermath of Hillsborough. But there are dozens, probably hundreds, of casualties still walking the streets of Merseyside. Parents, relatives, friends of those who lost their lives have been scarred for the rest of their lives ... youngsters who are growing up without their fathers, who were lost at Hillsborough.

Carl Rimmer was nineteen and had been dating a local girl called Alex for a number of years. I was his favourite player. He lost his life watching me and the team in that FA Cup Semi-Final. I will never forget that, and sometimes it is hard not to feel a sense of guilt. A few days after Hillsborough, Ronnie Whelan and I went to his house to comfort his parents. We were both apprehensive, we wondered how we would be received, whether we could actually do anything useful. But we knew it was important to go, and we wanted to do whatever we could do. We were both surprised by their reaction. Carl's parents made us feel so welcome, they were such lovely people. They appreciated us being there, and we felt as if we were doing something positive, making an effective contribution in helping them when they needed it. They were such polite, gentle people, they even asked me to get permission from Liverpool Football Club, so they could lay a bouquet on The Kop where Carl used to stand. I could hardly believe it, that was the least I could do. Half of Carl's ashes have been laid on The Kop, the other cast in a memorial stone at the Crematorium. Now Ted and Doreen Rimmer and Alex have become close friends of our family. We go out together. Julie and I know the torment they have been through.

Carl and his brother Kevin went to Hillsborough with two tickets, one for the stands, and one for the Leppings Lane terraces. Although Kevin is the eldest, Carl is the bigger, so Carl went on to the terraces while Kevin went into the stands. They arranged to meet on a hill near the ground shortly after the match ended. Kevin stood on the hill for two hours waiting anxiously for Carl.

Carl never showed. The next time Kevin saw his brother was in the makeshift morgue at Hillsborough. He was Number 15 in a room full of bodies. When Carl's family came to Anfield for counselling, Julie got them a signed Liverpool shirt. On the back was Number 15. When we first went out together, we went for a meal. We sat down at the table in this restaurant, it was at table Number 15.

Carl's sister was due to get married four weeks after Hillsborough, but Ted and Doreen naturally wanted to call it off, and so did Carl's sister. She just couldn't face getting married so soon after Carl's death; she did not know how to cope with the prospect of trying to enjoy herself with Carl's death on her mind as well as the whole of the family's.

Even so, they went ahead with the wedding. Julie and I were invited. It started off in an extremely strange atmosphere, no one really knew how to react, and Carl was not just at the back of everyone's minds, he was in the forefront, as all the guests expected he would be. But, by 1 a.m. we were all singing and dancing and it turned out to be a wonderful night for Carl's sister and the whole of the family.

Ever since that night we have gone out on a regular basis, and Ted invited us out for his birthday in Southport. It was Carl's birthday on 15 February when he would have been 20, and Ted and Doreen rang us on the day . . .

The Hillsborough Family Support Group are still operational on Merseyside, and many people are still in need of counselling.

We heard of one lad who was in the Leppings Lane crush and who survived, but was never quite the same after it, and in fact acted quite strange. There was a TV documentary about

Hillsborough almost a year after the event, showing a minute-by-minute breakdown of how it all happened. The next day he committed suicide. No one really can be sure whether the TV documentary triggered off the suicide, but I spoke to his brother who was disgusted that the programme should have been shown at all. To many it would have been viewed as an excellent piece of TV coverage of an event of national importance, but not to this lad's family.

Something like that leaves a sour taste, and it's not the only thing. I was appalled that the FA rejected the personal appeal from Trevor Hicks, Chairman of the Hillsborough Family Support Group for the FA Cup to go to the City of Liverpool as a permanent memorial. Equally, I was disgusted that the FA reduced the allocation for Cup Final tickets to 20,000 per club after their efforts to make the 1989 Cup Final the Memorial Final by giving it over to the fans with an allocation of 36,000 per club.

However, there have also been things that have touched me. Trevor and Jenni Hicks' two daughters were lost at Hillsborough. When they discovered I was compiling this book they sent me photographs that their daughter Vicki had taken of me when she was twelve, and her match reports of the games in which I have played, plus a biography of me.

In remembrance of Vicki Hicks and her sister, Sarah, I would like to reproduce in full her immaculately typewritten description of her favourite Liverpool player that took pride of place in her scrap-book.

Steve McMahon, known to his team-mates and in The Kop as 'Macker' is a Scouser born and bred. As a boy he was ball-boy at Goodison Park and graduated through the ranks there to make his debut (in the first team) for Everton in

1980. He went on to make 119 appearances for Everton before signing for Aston Villa in May 1983 for a fee of £300,000. He was offered the chance to play for Liverpool, but being an Everton fan as a boy opted to play for Aston Villa.

However, in the early stages of the 1985–86 season he didn't need asking twice when Liverpool again offered him the chance to play for them, so for a fee of £325,000 he became Kenny Dalglish's first new recruit after becoming manager. He made his debut for Liverpool on 14 September 1985 against Oxford United and scored the winner in the game the following week against Everton. However, in the crucial last weeks of the season Steve had to drop out of the side due to injury and was only substitute in the FA Cup Final.

Steve has had to take a bit of stick from his team-mates since he arrived at Anfield, and not just because he used to play for Everton. It all started around the time that Liverpool met QPR in the semi-final of the Milk Cup. His team-mates ended up calling him a jinx and pointed out that he had spent a considerable amount of time at Goodison Park yet it wasn't until he left that Everton began to win things. Then his second club, Aston Villa who had maintained their trophy-a-year sequence for many seasons, didn't win anything while he was there. So when Steve went to Anfield and Liverpool were knocked out by QPR, his team-mates blamed it all on him. However, he went on to have the last laugh as Liverpool won the Double.

Steve isn't really superstitious but he likes to go onto the pitch fourth in line. Steve rooms with Jan Molby and like Jan he likes to get his quota of sleep because his two young children keep him awake during the week. Travelling to away games Steve joins in the card school, and his pre-match meal is the usual steak, beans, tea and toast. His captain says that he can size up a situation with a humorous comment. He's a shy, quiet person but very funny and easily makes his team-mates laugh. Apart from football Steve enjoys a game of snooker and golf. Once he went with Alan Hansen and Gary Gillespie to play in a golfing tournament but it didn't turn out to be his day. He bought himself a new pair of white golf shoes which he took with him to Anfield and someone stood on them, leaving big stud marks across the top of them. Then it took him more than four hours to get through the first few holes.

When Steve first came to Liverpool he played in the No. 7 shirt but is now the anchorman in midfield wearing the No. 11 shirt. He's said to have extremely good vision so is a good passer of the ball as well as having a good shot. This season (1986–87) he is the leading goal-scorer in the Littlewoods Challenge Cup.

Marvellous for the age of twelve, and a girl at that! I've read a lot worse from some of the top sports writers! Not only that, but Vicki always seemed to have a good word for me in her 'match-reports' and her dad Trevor picked out a few for me. Liverpool 0, Spurs 1, 11 October 1986, Vicki was neat and precise with her 'reports': 'Liverpool's Steve McMahon had an especially good game with many shots and good passes from start to finish. One shot in particular was pure brilliance. It was a full-blooded shot that had so much power in it that it half knocked Clemence over.' Not bad, considering we lost!

Liverpool 10, Fulham 0, Littlewoods Cup 2nd round, 1st leg, Tuesday, 23 September 1986: 'By half-time the score was 4–0 after both McMahon and Whelan had scored brilliant goals.

Fulham's goalkeeper made some brilliant saves which included saving a penalty from Steve McMahon. Liverpool soon hit top gear again with Wark and McMahon making it 6–0. McMahon soon scored a hat-trick and took the score past the previous highest score in the history of the competition. By the 80th minute of the match McMahon, Rush, and Nicol had scored to make the final score 10–0. McMahon, who was obviously the game's hero, left the pitch clutching the match ball. When interviewed he said: "It was tremendous scoring my first hat-trick in senior football, especially as I missed a penalty as well!"'

I'm sure my England World Cup colleague Paul Parker won't forgive me for reminding him of this match as he was playing in the Fulham defence! Just to rub it in, here is the second leg, Fulham 2, Liverpool 3, aggregate score 13–2: 'Steve McMahon, who scored four times [I wish I had, but I missed a penalty], hammered home a 20-yard blast. Five minutes later McMahon was on the attack again, this time with an inch perfect pass that Parker, who was trying to hold off Rush, slid into his own net.'

Lord Justice Taylor's report has called for stadiums to become all-seater within four years. Fine, but I don't see the issue of all-seater stadiums as the most important. There have been many big games, like our FA Cup Semi-Final with Nottingham Forest, over the years, with fans standing on the terraces without any major tragedies like the one at Hillsborough. I see no reason to dispose of The Kop or the Stretford end. There has never been any problems at Anfield or Old Trafford, or any of the big grounds. In my view there have been big mistakes made and the authorities should hold up their hands and admit that they got it wrong – that's the FA and the police.

Chapter 6

Club Bosses: Dalglish, Kendall

I HAVE THE DISTINCTION of being Kenny Dalglish's first signing in his career in management, and for that reason I suppose I am as well qualified as anyone to know the real manager of Liverpool FC.

Dalglish has a mystique as a manager, as the public don't really know him, but the reality is far removed from the image. Kenny is such a character, a fabulous bloke, but he doesn't portray himself that way to the supporters or the media. Kenny is far more at ease on the training pitch and in the environment of the football club. Football, and Liverpool FC in particular, is his life. In that respect he reminds me of Gordon Lee, my first manager at Everton.

Kenny is in control when he is working at Anfield. He is at ease there, and he enjoys himself. He is a hard-working manager, often out very late, as he sees a lot of games, watches a lot of players.

He is certainly his own man. Most managers announce their team on Friday after training, telling their players to allow them to build themselves up for the match 24 hours later. Not Kenny. From his very first game as manager, his policy was to announce his team in the dressing-rooms an hour before the kick-off. The players were not accustomed to it, and naturally take time to adjust to anything new like this. Kenny takes his squad into the dressing-room, shuts the door, everybody sits down and he goes through the line-up of the day. If he has decided to shake up the side for any reason, any player left out will be told individually before the team selection ceremony in the dressing-rooms. He will tell you privately, but won't necessarily tell you the reasons. If you want to know why, any player is at liberty to thrash out their differences with the manager on Monday morning. He has proved that he is no respecter of reputations, having left out England World Cup striker Peter Beardsley on occasions – and the manager paid a record at the time £1.9 million for him!

Kenny is very methodical. He has dossiers on the opposition, and he goes through each player in detail before each match. It's a hallmark of Liverpool FC that everyone at the club does their homework. In training, on occasions, Kenny might go through the routine of our opponents' set pieces, that is their strengths at corners and free kicks, and possibly work on certain moves they may have. Sometimes Kenny would go through these in great detail, sometimes not.

He has his set match routine. Whether we are playing home or away, he tends to take us to a hotel for an overnight stay to prepare for the game, so that we are away from family and friends without any distractions. We would normally arrive at the hotel at around 5.30 p.m., with an evening meal arranged for 6.30 p.m. We are at liberty to choose whatever we want to eat a night before a match, and the lads would usually start with a soup, either mushroom or tomato, followed by a main course of chicken, fish or steak (the favourite among the lads), accompanied by beans, mash and peas. Of course, that applies to all the players – except Bruce Grobbelaar. Our goalkeeper will always have a bash at something just a little different, such as veal in garlic sauce — perhaps, fried cobra on toast! Clearly he doesn't suffer with overnight nerves or he has a constitution of steel. The rest of us, well we don't mind the normal food. We don't really get bored with it, after all it's only once a week. We're all tucked up in our beds by 9 p.m. Roy Evans will go from room to room to ensure that we are all asleep. Anyone struggling to nod off will be given sleeping tablets, and there are a couple who do take them. Kenny puts a great deal of reliance on a good night's sleep the night before a match. Whatever the manager wants, he gets from his players.

Kenny Dalglish commanded enormous respect from the very first day he became Liverpool manager. That respect emanated from his achievements in the game. He was a masterly performer, one of the greatest players of all time, not just in the British Isles but the world. He also commanded respect because of the kind of person he is, dedicated to the game. We all have our faults, but professionally no one can fault Kenny for his commitment to the cause of winning trophies for Liverpool FC.

One of the secrets of Kenny Dalglish and every Liverpool manager is that they do not have any problems apart from finding the right team to win matches. Everything else is left to the highly efficient back-room staff, where everyone specializes in the smooth running of a successful club.

For example, I signed a six-year contract with Liverpool, one of the longest ever signed by the current playing squad at Anfield. The contract was negotiated by the club's chief executive, Peter Robinson. He handles the contracts of all the players as well as the finances involved in transfers of players. The manager dictates the players he wants to sign and Peter Robinson negotiates the price. The manager decides which players he wants retained on contract and, again, the chief executive sorts out the finances and the documentation. Kenny would say to the people 'upstairs' that these are the players I want to keep at the club and it's up to you how far you want to go in terms of finance to keep them. A football club has become more complex than it used to be and a manager needs to be free to concentrate on team affairs. It is a system that has worked perfectly at Anfield over many years now, and one that has been copied by other clubs both big and small.

Not only has Kenny Dalglish made me his first signing as manager, he has also recommended that the club sign me now on a six-year contract, a very important contract for me at this stage of my career. It takes me up to a testimonial at Liverpool and effectively ties me to the club for the rest of my playing career, unless of course the club wish to sell me, which is their prerogative as it is with any player on the staff. But, I have the security of a six-year contract, and that brings peace of mind which can only help me to produce my best for the team and the club.

I suppose it's unusual that I've actually played with my manager at Liverpool and my manager at Everton! When Kenny Dalglish first took charge of team affairs at Liverpool he was still very much active as a player. When Howard Kendall arrived at Everton he managed a handful of games as player-manager . . .

By the time Howard Kendall walked through the doors at Goodison, he had already made his mark in management at Blackburn. Like most new brooms in this game, they tend to sweep a soccer club clean. Howard arrived with his own ideas and it wasn't long before players were coming and going at regular intervals. He bought seven players, and they became known as the Magnificent Seven. Among them were goalkeeper Neville Southall, Mickey Walsh, Alan Biley, Alan Ainscow and big Mick Ferguson.

One of Howard's greatest attributes as a manager is his ability to get on so well with his players. Equally, he has a ruthless streak when he needs it. Half-way through my first season with Everton I badly damaged my knee and spent the rest of the season building myself up and working in conjunction with Gordon Lee. The first game of the following season, I wasn't quite fit, so I played in the reserves. Everton kicked off the new League season with a marvellous 3–1 win at Birmingham, while I played in the reserves' 4–0 win against Bolton. I thought I would have to wait for my chance to get back into the side, but I was shocked, when, on the Wednesday, he drafted me into the first team squad and dropped Trevor Ross, picking me in his place. I can imagine that Trevor felt pretty aggrieved by that, particularly as he had played so well in such an exceptional team performance. That, as one might guess, was my first experience of Howard Kendall's ruthless streak. It wasn't to be my last!

The parting of the ways between Howard and myself was not the most amicable. I left Everton at the end of my contract, which, of course, I was perfectly entitled to do. However, there was every chance that I could have stayed at Goodison. At the time, Everton were not doing very well, but Howard insisted that he had made every effort to persuade me to stay and suggested he had made me the biggest contract offer ever made by the club. I was puzzled because that simply wasn't the case. I'd been nominated Player-of-the-Year at the club, yet I got the impression that the final decision to let me go was not taken solely by the manager. I just had this feeling that maybe the Board of Directors wanted to cash in on my transfer. Whatever the truth behind it all, I signed for Aston Villa.

Ironically, Aston Villa went on an end-of-season break to Magaluf, and I went with them – and ended up at the same location as Everton as they had gone on the same vacation! We had a chat while we were together out in Portugal . . . if you can call it a chat. There were a lot of things I could have said, but I didn't. I bit my lip. I came to the conclusion that they had already decided to sell me and that's why he had offered me a contract that I knew wasn't as good an offer as some of the other players given new deals at the same time. But we were all out there relaxing and enjoying ourselves; it was not a time to pick an argument, and in any case when I left Goodison, Howard had said to me: 'OK, I think you have made the wrong decision in going, but good luck.'

The perfect example of his ruthless streak emerged when Mick Walsh and Billy Wright had been given free transfers at Everton, as well as a few other players, at the same time that I left to join Villa. Yet Howard Kendall took both Walsh and Wright with the Everton team to Magaluf! It goes without saying that the pair of them were pretty bitter about being shown the door by Howard, yet there they were on holiday with him.

One of Howard Kendall's strengths, in his view, was to do a bit of socializing with the players to get us close to him. But there is a logic to it. Howard would take out his players on a fairly regular basis, even when he had returned from an away game after suffering a heavy defeat. He would tell his team: 'Phone the wife, or the girlfriend and tell them you will be at least an hour or so late getting back, I'm taking you all for a drink in the pub – the drinks are on me!' That kind of approach always went down well with his players, as you might expect. But his philosophy, I would imagine, is that a few drinks in the pub loosens the tongues and he likes to know exactly what his players are thinking and saying on a wide variety of subjects, but particularly about each other, the club and the manager. In that respect he is a good manager in my book, an example of how to handle his players.

Chapter 7

Liverpool's Mighty Men

BLUE, VENNERS, BUGSY, Stick, Jockey, Hiso, Abbo, The Ferret, Billy, Vitch, Chiko, Digger, Tosh, Modo, Shekel, Yank, Stan.

The Boss strides into the Liverpool team dressing-room, sits everybody down and rattles off the names ... in goal Blue, right-back Venners, left-back Chiko, centre-backs The Stick and Jockey, in midfield The Ferret, Billy, Vitch, and up-front Digger, Tosh and Modo. That, for argument's sake, might be the team that The Gaffer or The Boss, Kenny Dalglish, will name. He rattles off the team by their nicknames. If someone new joins the club, like Ronnie Rosenthal, he must wonder what team the Liverpool manager has named here! By now Ronnie Rosenthal is better known as Shekel, and knows precisely whom the Liverpool manager means.

The Liverpool squad is renowned for its strength in depth and is one of the reasons why we'll always start a season as most people's favourites for at least one of the major prizes, if not two, or even three. And it's sheer delight to run through the number of top-quality players we have at Anfield, revealing the inside secrets as to their pet names.

Let's start with manager **Kenny Dalglish**, whom we all respect. We call him The Boss or The Gaffer, but he can mix in with the rest of us, he's game for a laugh and we're not frightened, on occasion, to call him by his nickname, 'Les'. He got that nickname because of a mix-up a couple of years ago when Kenny was calling this fellow Les by mistake; he had got the names completely wrong so we started to call him Les and it's stuck ever since. It's silly really but that's how these names begin.

Bruce Grobbelaar   Well, his nickname is Blue, but don't ask me why, I haven't a clue. Over the years he has become one of Liverpool's best goalkeepers in their history. He is also one of the great characters of the game. Liverpool can be proud of their goalkeeping tradition with players of the calibre of Ray Clemence and Tommy Lawrence, but I'd put Brucie at the top. I know that he would love to play for England and I'm sure he would do well although he is used to being a Liverpool keeper.

The Liverpool goalkeepers have to be a little bit special, a little bit different, they are almost an extra defender, roaming out of the penalty box and performing a kind of sweeper's job. Brucie is talented enough, not only to perform that role for Liverpool, but adapt to international level and play his part for England. The problem has been that he has represented Zimbabwe in the past and is ineligible to play for England. He feels desperately frustrated that he is missing out when all the lads go off for international duty, not just with England, but with Scotland, the Republic of Ireland, Northern Ireland, Sweden, Denmark and even Wales!

Brucie is such a good goalkeeper that he doesn't deserve to be left behind and feel the odd one out, virtually training on his own when we all leave him during international week. His main attributes are his extraordinary agility; he makes things look easy, as if they are no problem at all. He can also do the unexpected, which is not always to the liking of the management and coaching staff. Sometimes he lacks a bit of concentration, and that's understandable, especially in our team where he doesn't get involved as much as he would if he were playing behind some other defence. At times his mind wanders off and he indulges in a little banter with the crowd, much to the annoyance of the manager.

But there is no mistaking his flamboyance, and few will forget his antics as he wobbled his legs before a vital penalty in the European Cup Final which put the player off enough to miss his penalty kick. It had a dual effect, as if to say 'I'm not frightened', and also, 'the onus is on you to score from the penalty'. It certainly had the desired psychological effect and won the European Cup for Liverpool.

Barry Venison is better known as Venners and he came to Anfield after writing to all the English First Division clubs when his contract had expired at Sunderland. I don't know how many clubs wrote back, but he got the required correspondence from the club he wanted, namely Liverpool. One day, in he came, the new boy, and sat next to me in the dressing-room, no doubt because there was a spare space beside me, once occupied by Craig Johnston, who shocked everyone by walking out of the club for private reasons. Craig could make you laugh, he had a tremendous sense of humour, he was a funny lad and it was an entirely different type of personality that replaced him in the dressing-room beside me. Barry is a quiet lad really, he doesn't say too much, but he has done well for Liverpool and that's all that's important.

Liverpool have an excellent tradition for exceptional full-backs; players seem to have blossomed in that position at this club and Barry is no exception, he has settled down well. There have been times when he has been left out and brought back in again. Despite his in-and-out status, he has still played a large number of games for someone still in his mid-twenties. He has a good head on his shoulders and is an outstanding reader of the game and has enough ability to make an impression. In fact, he played in the centre of midfield for Sunderland, emphasizing that he can pass the ball with extreme accuracy.

David Burrows   Naturally enough, known as Bugsy, and is Liverpool's left-back despite tremendous competition from outstanding players like Steve Staunton and Gary Abblet. Bugsy joined us from West Bromwich Albion as a young lad, but from the moment he arrived at Anfield we were all convinced that he was an outstanding prospect. Any young player coming to a club like Anfield has to go through the learning process in the first twelve months and it's no surprise that most of them find it difficult to adjust to the pace of our game. But Bugsy is such a quick player, and an accomplished one, that he was able to come through his first year emerging as a powerful contender for the left-back position.

He is already an England Under-21 international, and as he gains confidence he could progress along the international ladder. He has a lot of competition at this club and I'm sure that will only serve to make him an even better player. He has a great deal of pace and he is a good tackler with a sweet left foot.

Steve Staunton is better known as Stan and he was unfortunate at the start of the new season as he suffered some injury problems which held back his progress. He has a great left foot: he can 'ping' a ball over distance with superb accuracy. He lacks a little bit of pace, but he makes up for that with being a good footballer with a good footballing brain.

Gary Abblet   Abbo can play at either left-back or centre-back, demonstrating his versatility. He has progressed in leaps and bounds, his confidence increasing, and with that his status in the team. He has done a superb job for the club; he is one of our unsung heroes, and has been for the last two seasons, switching his role without complaint. The club almost sold him at one time, and he was on loan to Derby County. Derby were very impressed with him but Liverpool insisted that he was only there on loan for the experience, and the club would not entertain a permanent move. I'm sure the loan spell at Derby helped him to blossom out and he's become a valuable member of the Liverpool squad.

Gary Gillespie   Well, he's known as The Stick and it's easy to see why, because he looks like a big stick! The competition is fierce in virtually every position at Liverpool but at centre-half there are some exceptional players, such as Glen Hysen and our skipper Alan Hansen. Gary has been really unfortunate, with a succession of injuries thoughout his spell at Liverpool. He is an easy-going, quiet, happy-go-lucky fellow and sometimes you sense when he does get injured he doesn't push himself hard enough to make sure he's right to get himself back in the team. Perhaps it's more of a psychological block, that he's worried that playing through injuries will only exacerbate the problem. But injuries are so commonplace in professional football that there are numerous players prepared to push themselves through games and take the risks. Personally, I'm one of those players who will push himself into the team and play despite injuries, providing of course it's physically possible to do so. I wouldn't say The Stick is a hypochondriac – it's just all in his head!

But he can be forgiven for all his injury worries because he is such an outstanding central defender, so stylish, so composed, so commanding in the air and, in many ways, he's a player in the mould of Alan Hansen. He can score goals, some vital ones, and in all seriousness it's a pity that over the years he has not steered clear of injuries.

Glen Hysen Better known to his team-mates as Hiso, he took his time to adjust to the pace of English football and to the style of the Liverpool team. He came to us with a reputation as being one of the best, if not the best, sweepers in European and world football. He was playing sweeper for Fiorentina, but when he arrived at Anfield he was asked to use his height and strength in a marker role. It was remarkable how well he adapted and even managed to counteract the strengths of Wimbledon in the air. It must have been difficult to make that switch but the fact that he did so well, underlines his enormous ability and strength in the air.

It was a great coup for Liverpool to sign him, as the club virtually pinched him from under the noses of Manchester United. Now, he loves the place and he is starting, just like Jan Molby, to pick up the Scouse accent. The fact that he has settled down so well has also helped him, but then again he couldn't have picked a better club to come to in this country, to help him adjust to English football.

Since Ossie Ardiles and Ricky Villa came to this country in 1978, there have been more than 100 imports and precious few have made much of an impact. There have been the two Dutchmen, Frans Thijssen and Arnold Muhren at Ipswich as well as the two Argentinians at Spurs, but otherwise the vast majority of our imported players have failed to live up to their reputations. Glen Hysen is one of those exceptions.

Alan Hansen Jockey is a natural name for a big Jock like Alan. He is so laid-back, sometimes he could be mistaken for being asleep! He has the perfect temperament both on and off the pitch – absolutely nothing seems to bother him. Over the years, he has been Liverpool's most outstanding player, and that says something in a team of so many exceptional stars. He has proved his pedigree, he has won virtually everything in the game, and he is still going strong at the age of 35. Just look how many games he has played, it's incredible. There have been so many stories that he has crippled knees and that he'd be finished, but he is defying all the rumours and playing on. To reach the age of 35 and still be playing in the First Division is a remarkable achievement for an outfield player.

I'm sure he is destined to join the succession of Anfield players who have switched successfully to the coaching staff. But Al has a few more years left on his contract and I'm convinced he'll want to play on for as long as humanly possible. Changes seem to happen out of the blue at Anfield and nothing that goes on there seems to surprise me any more. All of a sudden, one day, I'll walk into the club and Al will be there in his track suit, as one of the coaches instead of one of the players. But I hope that doesn't happen for a long time because we'd miss a player of such remarkable composure. His main attributes are his ability to come out of defence with the ball, creating so much space for others in the team. He can be dangerous coming from the back and has so much control and skill that players like myself in midfield just move out of the way and let him go through.

What's more, to add to all his enormous talent as a player, he is an excellent golfer. I'm sure he could have been a professional golfer rather than a professional footballer, and he probably wishes he'd turned to golf where there's far more money these days! I know I won the golf tournament among the players in the World Cup Finals in Italy, but I only did it because Al wasn't around. He's too good for me on the golf-course; I'm not in his league. It's a good job he's not English!

Billy is a nickname of yours truly and there lies a long story. One day I went along to a pro-am golf tournament with several of my team-mates in Leeds. When we arrived we were each told that we had been sponsored individually and the tournament organizers read out our names and our affiliated sponsor. It went something like this: 'Alan Hansen – Bradford and Bingley. Gary Gillespie – Leeds Building Society. Steve Nicol – Leeds Metalwork.' And then, they shouted out my name last with – Billy Ingham and Friends. Then, all of a sudden, we spotted Billy Ingham and his friends – and Billy Ingham was 4ft. 6in. and all of his friends were 4ft. 6in. It was so funny with our sponsors carting all our golf gear around and Billy Ingham and friends all under 5ft. They carted my stuff around for about five and a half hours, they were so slow, and all the lads were rolling about with laughter. Ever since then the name of Billy has stuck. The lads who had been at the golf tournament with me took great pleasure in relating the story to everyone else once they got back to Anfield.

Ronnie Whelan   He's known as Vitch and even though he's my room-mate, I haven't a clue why they call him that. He's a great lad, very down to earth, and I'd better duck when I now reveal what we really call him, and that's The Skunk. He's the smelliest person you've ever met in the world and he doesn't suffer from sweat or BO. I'll have to leave it to your imagination to work out just why he smells so much! It's unfortunate for me because I have to spend so much of the time with him and when he's not smelling the room out he's got his head buried in a book and I might as well be on my own. He loves true stories, and once he opens a book that's the last you'll hear of him for the rest of the evening.

Whatever he does off the field, on it he's an outstanding player and wears the No. 5 shirt for Liverpool even though he plays in midfield. Ray Kennedy wore the No. 5 shirt before him and he, too, was a midfield player. I wear the No. 11 shirt and I'm also a midfield player. You just pick up the shirt that you're given and I suppose I was handed the No. 11 shirt as I was taking over from Graeme Souness in the Liverpool team.

Perhaps it's all about superstition, that it's the traditional thing at Anfield to wear your predecessor's shirt number. Everyone is very superstitious at the club. If you do something one week, no matter how trivial or seemingly inconsequential, it has to be done every week until the team is beaten. Someone might smack you on the back of the head and you win a game, and they're smacking you on the back of the head every week! Our coach, Ronnie Moran, found a silver coin on our training pitch at the start of last season and he said he would keep hold of it until the end of the season to bring us luck; it certainly brought us luck and he's kept it ever since.

As for Ronnie Whelan, it says an awful lot for him that at such a marvellously successful club as Liverpool he has been a permanent fixture in the team for the past ten years. He must be a great player. He is the club's vice captain, understudy to Alan Hansen, and if they are both missing for whatever reason I'm next in line as skipper. He's a very honest player, works very hard, a player you always like to have alongside you in the team.

Ray Houghton Better known as The Ferret, and I suppose he has got that name because he's such a busy type of player, always ferreting around. His work-rate is phenomenal: he always wants to be involved in the action, he just never stops.

Although he is a busy player, the prerequisites of fitting into the Liverpool set-up are the basic principles of the game of being able to pass the ball and having the fundamental techniques and skills. I'm sure that when the scouts go out to watch a prospective Liverpool player the questions they ask are, 'Can he pass the ball?', and, 'Can he play?'. If they can perform both basic functions, the player has a chance of fitting into the type of team framework at Liverpool. Ray has been a wonderful success with us and it is remarkable that he was given a free transfer by West Ham, and had to resurrect his career at Fulham before joining Oxford from where he was transferred to Liverpool.

The oddity about The Ferret is that one minute you think you're talking to a Cockney, the next to a Jock. Basically he's a Jock who's been brought up in London – and that's why he plays for the Republic of Ireland! We have a good mixture of lads at Anfield and Ray is one of the fairly quiet ones.

Steve Nicol We call him Chiko and once again I haven't a clue why, but once these nicknames stick they never go away. Steve is an outstanding, versatile player whose best position is left-back, but he can play at right-back and in midfield. I feel his best position is at left-back where he is able to go forward, creating havoc in opponents' defences, and quite capable of scoring plenty of goals. Even though he's an exceptional talent, he has to be at his best, like everyone else, to keep his place in the team. You simply cannot afford to have a bad game or you risk losing your place and that applies to even the most talented of players.

Jan Molby The Yank, a mixture of Jan and Molby, and he just loves to be considered a Scouser. You'd think he had been born and bred in Liverpool. In fact, the funny thing is he's probably more Scouse than I am! Not only did he pick up the language very quickly but he's got the local accent off to a tee. He's a very intelligent lad and, as well as mastering the English language, he speaks German as well. He's been linked with moves to Glasgow Rangers and other clubs, but why would he want to leave the best club in Europe? I suppose you can understand the fact that he could be unsettled because he's not been a regular in the team lately and Glasgow Rangers are a big club. No one as talented as Jan can be satisfied with being a reserve. He is so skilful he can walk past defenders with sheer ability, he doesn't need pace. He can pass the ball over long distances with remarkable accuracy. He is an expert in the sweeper role because he is such an intelligent player but he prefers to play in midfield.

John Barnes Appropriately enough, we call him Digger, after the character in Dallas. Digger is an intelligent lad and also has a fantastic sense of humour – he can be very funny indeed. He came to Anfield as only the second black player at the club after Howard Gayle. Opposing fans, especially Evertonians and at derby matches, gave him some stick, throwing bananas and chanting their insults. It doesn't happen nearly as much now, mainly because Digger just ignored it; it was water off a duck's back, he has thick skin. We all know that racial abuse goes on in football but in certainly doesn't bother him. In fact, he finds it quite amusing.

He has fitted in superbly well in the Liverpool team. It's a pity he cannot produce his marvellous skills consistently in an England shirt; many have wondered why he can't and I don't have any ready-made answers either. However, in the Liverpool team, as soon as anyone gets the ball they always look to play it to John Barnes. Certainly, I do. He's such a gifted, dangerous player that I feel it essential to get the ball to him as quickly as possible and let him take on the full-back. That doesn't happen so readily with England, a team packed full of individuals who want to do their bits and pieces on the ball and make their own impression.

John Barnes finds himself isolated at times on the left wing playing for his country, with possession limited, particularly in comparison to the amount of the ball he gets in the Liverpool side. I fully appreciate that he has played over 50 internationals and people expect a lot of him but they tend to forget that, in international terms, he is still relatively young at the age of 26. I know he didn't have as potent a World Cup as he wanted but I find it extraordinary that opposing supporters should now start to boo him. That's exceptionally hard on the lad, he doesn't deserve it. We all hoped he would make an impact in Italy but he struggled with injuries. I don't agree with those who feel his contribution was negligible. His mere presence was a contribution in itself because the opposition needed two defenders to mark him and that created space for others.

Personally, I'd keep faith with John Barnes in the England set-up and I am sure that would be the feeling of new England manager, Graham Taylor. The attitude here at Anfield is that we're interested first and foremost in how well he does for Liverpool and, in all honesty, no one here is particularly bothered if he fails to make the same impact with England, as long as he is successful in the Liverpool team. However, I believe in John Barnes and that he will eventually prove to be a valuable asset for his country as well as his club.

I would hope that John Barnes stays in English football and is not lost to our game, but I would have to say that it looks likely that he will leave at the end of his contract which expires at the end of this season. He has always harboured an ambition to play on the Continent, and if he goes he will be missed.

But Liverpool have lost monumental talents over the years and it's never seemed to damage the club's effectiveness in winning major honours. The names change but the team doesn't. It just seems to carry on, and the club somehow manages to find replacements. When Ian Rush was sold to Juventus there were huge question marks about whether the team would survive. Who could replace Rushie? That was the question on everyone's lips when he went to Italy. Yet, the manager, Kenny Dalglish, went out and bought John Barnes from Watford for £900,000 and Peter Beardsley from Newcastle for £1.9 million and we enjoyed a magnificent season without the club's star striker.

Graeme Souness was another player who everyone thought

would be virtually impossible to replace, and I would agree that he was a hard act to follow because I was the one who had to do it. But I didn't treat it as if I was following in the footsteps of a truly great player for Liverpool, I didn't treat it like that in any way. I was determined to be myself, play the way I knew best and do whatever I could to prove that Graeme Souness would not be missed.

I didn't have a Graeme Souness complex when I first came to Liverpool. I consider myself a totally different player who can make an impression and an impact in my own right, particularly in such a good team. I can't blame people for comparing me with Graeme Souness, and my only reaction to that is that it is a compliment to be compared with such a great player. Should John Barnes go, then Kenny Dalglish will probably find a young player who could be just as good and as effective.

But John Barnes has been one of the outstanding players in the country in recent years – and certainly for his club. He has magnificent ball control, and a great left foot. He can make things happen if the team is struggling, he can be a match-winner, he can unlock the door when the game is deadlocked. He has superb close control, he can put the ball on a tanner, his dribbling ability is a joy to behold. On top of that, he's a lovely person and even a good singer, making all our rap records.

Ian Rush We call him Tosh, no doubt after John Toshack, another Welshman, who was magnificent in the air. I suppose we're taking the micky out of Rushie, who is not as adept as big Tosh was as far as heading the ball is concerned.

When he first came to Anfield he found it quite difficult to settle in; it was a big challenge for him, mainly because he was coming from a small-time town like Chester and he was a shy lad. When I first saw him he was very much in his shell, but now there's no stopping him! Now that he's cast off his shyness we find him to be a very funny lad. We're always having a go at him and he's always having a go back. We rib him about being a Welsh international star, because he's the only one not going to any World Cups. In the past, he would have taken offence but now he snaps back.

It's almost a nonsense asking the question, 'What is Rush's main attribute?' He scores goals. He does that because he's so quick, and his phenomenal speed enables him to get into potential scoring positions. A lot of the time he makes his own goals, he doesn't need them laid on a plate. The new offside rule where a player is not deemed offside when he's level with the last defender can only benefit strikers who rely on their speed like Rushie and Gary Lineker.

Peter Beardsley I hope he'll forgive me for divulging his nickname, Modo, after Quasimodo. It's not a very flattering nickname but a lot of nicknames are meant to be derogatory. You've got to take it in the way it's meant and Peter does exactly that, he accepts it in good fun. Basically, he's a quiet lad and he's the Anfield fact file. He's the quiz master in our own game of Question of Sport and he certainly knows his stuff. If we ask any questions ourselves, Peter Beardsley's the man to get them right. The main challengers to his crown are John Barnes and Gary Abblet. John Barnes has an incredible knowledge of foreign sports.

Peter Beardsley is a busy type of player with quicksilver feet and tricky skills, enabling him to beat two or three defenders in a small area. Like John Barnes, he can unlock the door and break the stalemate in any match. The team changed its style slightly when Rushie left and was replaced by Barnes and Beardsley. Now that Rushie is back, he likes an early pass to fulfil all his goal potential. Although players like John Barnes and Peter Beardsley sometimes like to hold a ball up and dribble, in the main everybody in the team knows that an early pass is most effective. Peter Beardsley is a difficult player for the opposition to mark because he's not just an out-and-out front man, he has the flexibility to move off the front line and play off the main striker.

Ronnie Rosenthal I think everyone would agree that his nickname of Shekel really needs no explanation for an Israeli international forward. He joined us from Standard Leige towards the end of last season and made an immediate impact, scoring some vital goals to help us on the way to the Championship. It was a remarkable start by any standards but particularly for not just a new boy, but for a foreign player as well. But, just like Glen Hysen, we try to make such players welcome from the very start. And, just like Jan Molby, he's trying to get a touch of the Scouse accent.

Chapter 8

Hard Men

GRAEME SOUNESS IS MY IDEA of a hard man, so too is Graham Roberts, especially during his days with Spurs, but not the likes of Vinny Jones. I had the misfortune of crossing swords with Graeme in a big way during my days with Aston Villa in the formative years of my career. Graeme and Kenny Dalglish still remind me of the day they got me sent off — the only time I've been dismissed in my entire career. I was 23, playing for Villa, and Souness was the Liverpool skipper. It was a real Scottish double act: an incident with Kenny got me booked, and Graeme finished off the job by getting me sent off. The pair of them still laugh and joke about it. Kenny says I got booked because I couldn't catch him as he was too quick for me, so I had to hold him back. The truth is that Kenny had that style of play of shielding the ball and backing into an opponent. In my view I was fouled, but the referee booked me! Later on I was in a tussle with Souness and, as I kicked the ball away, he kicked me in the shin with his studs showing. I squared up to him and was sent off.

It's fascinating to look back and see that, at the time, I was quoted as saying: 'If anyone should have gone off, it should have

been Souness. He went over the top, it was as plain as anything
– I've got the stud marks on my shin to prove it. I didn't take a
swing at him. I just pushed him away, that's all. It was a
diabolical decision to send me off.'

In the same *Sunday Mirror* article Souness actually apologized!
He said: 'I'm sorry it happened. The last thing I want is anyone
sent off. The only mistake I made was to try and take a free
kick quickly in the last few seconds. He came in and tried to stop
me.'

Graeme and I were involved in some bruising battles when I
was at Everton and we clashed in Merseyside derby games. In
the mould of Dave Mackay, he was hard but fair. During our
tussles he'd not complain when he was on the receiving end of a
tackle, and I wouldn't complain when I felt the full force of one
of Graeme's tackles. We shared the same sort of hard man's
motto, if you like; if someone whacks you, you accept it, get up
and get on with the game, and wait for your chance to whack
them back.

Graham Roberts was always a 'fairly determined' character,
quite hard in the tackle. But I never had any cause to complain
whenever we clashed in midfield. There were never any confronta-
tions. In fact, we roomed together when we played for the England
B team. I like my sleep in the afternoon before a night game and no
sooner had we got back into the room, I got my head down and
went straight to sleep. Obviously, Graham didn't share my
enthusiasm for sleep. When I woke around 5 p.m. I was shocked to
discover Graham sitting there on the end of my bed – cleaning my
boots! I was even more stunned when I found out he had cleaned
all my boots, even polished them! I suppose I could have asked him
to clean my shoes as well, but that would have been taking a
liberty. Sorry, Graham, I'm only joking. I dare not offend him in
case I get him angry when I meet him next time on a soccer field.

Alan Ball was my hero as a lad. One of my greatest thrills was meeting him at the 1988 FA Cup Final when he was playing in an all-star match for an old England team against Scotland. I watched him, and afterwards he came over with his son Paul. He told me, 'You're my lad's favourite player!' I told him, 'That's funny — because you were my favourite player.'

When I stood on the Goodison terraces and watched Alan Ball, I said to myself he was the type of player I wanted to be. I must have been about thirteen years old when I bought those Alan Ball white boots that were all the craze at the time.

Early in my career with Everton I played against Alan, and no one really knows how happy I was to be on the same field, in the same company as him. Now I have achieved a few things and I have more to achieve. Though I began my career wanting to be like Ball, I feel I have evolved into my own type of player. Yet, there are a lot of similarities. Most striking is the will to win, and the importance of always doing your best and working hard. I have a hunger for success. Ball had it. That's what I thrive on.

But I consider myself as far more than just the kicker that, no doubt, rival fans may see me as and some of my critics describe me as. I don't really mean to kick anybody, but I do like to get involved. I certainly don't like to be considered a kicker, or a destroyer, as I believe I can play the game. When I first set out, my ideals were to be a creative midfield player, capable of stopping goals by defensive work and scoring them by attacking — really a bit of everything, an all-rounder.

Many people have compared me with Graeme Souness, naturally enough as I was bought to take over his role at Liverpool. But we are two different types of player. He's got his own style, although we both do like to stamp a little bit of authority on a game.

Every team has a hard man, and I should know, I normally come into direct contact with them in the midfield. Midfield is the engine-room of the team and will normally have one play maker and one ball winner; sometimes a team is lucky enough to have a player who can combine the two. The best are in the First Division, naturally, and here's my run-down of the best in the business.

Arsenal Actually, the Gunners' tough players are at the back, and Tony Adams springs to mind. He doesn't get a lot of credit; in fact, he gets quite a bit of stick from opposing fans who goad him with those 'donkey' jibes. But, believe me, when it comes to the tackle he doesn't mess about. Kevin Richardson was one of the most underrated midfield players in the League until George Graham sold him to Real Sociedad to link up with my old Anfield team-mate, John Aldridge. But I wouldn't say 'Rico' is tough. He does a superb job, and his best asset is his passing ability. My England colleague, David Rocastle, is a powerful player and can tackle and work hard, particularly for someone who usually plays wide on the right-hand side of midfield. He isn't an out-and-out winger, but he is strong as well as skilful.

Aston Villa Paul McGrath is as tough as they come. He plays centre-back but can also play in midfield and does so regularly for the Republic of Ireland. I didn't confront him in the European Championships in West Germany because I was one of the England substitutes and didn't come on. Now, McGrath *is* a hard player, and he likes winning — at all costs. Manchester United made a big mistake in selling him to Villa. That may have been one of the main reasons behind Villa's phenomenal transformation under Graham Taylor. I must own up and admit that I was surprised that Villa made such an impact in the Championship race, because last season everyone at Anfield, myself included, expected our greatest threat to emerge from title holders Arsenal,

Everton, and even Manchester United. It shows you how wrong you can be!

Charlton   All credit to Lennie Lawrence, he has relied on good football to keep Charlton in the First Division for as long as he could. It's a shame that they have failed to pull off their usual Houdini act. Tommy Caton has been a very good player in his time, making a big impression as a youngster at Manchester City before moving on to Arsenal. Similarly, Steve McKenzie has been an outstanding youngster. But Charlton don't have a nasty streak in their side.

Chelsea   Here's a club that has always had a hard man in their side from the days of Ron 'Chopper' Harris. There's been David Speedie, Graham Roberts, and don't forget Peter Nicholas. He has been around and has done his fair bit of kicking. He can be vicious when he wants to be, but he met his match in Graeme Souness. Nicholas tried to 'do' Souness in a tackle and it hurt our Liverpool skipper, but he waited patiently for his opportunity the next time their paths crossed on the football field. In the first 10 minutes Nicholas was off with a gashed shin, courtesy of Souness. Souness was not a player to be crossed on the field – he was the master at picking the time for retribution.

Coventry   David Speedie is a fiery little Scottish . . . whatever! I've confronted him many times on a football field but, whatever happens, we've got up, dusted ourselves down and shaken hands. No quarter asked, or given. We've exchanged a few swear words in the heat of the battle, words I wouldn't like to repeat! Plenty of verbal abuse goes on between competitive, combative players, but with someone like Speedie it's done to see how someone like myself might react. But I don't give them the satisfaction of reacting. Wimbledon have been the worst club for their players dishing out the verbal venom. John Fashanu was one of the main culprits and a few of his pals would join in. It could become quite ugly. But that would never happen with Speedie, it would never get out of control, and at the end of our battles it has always been no hard feelings and 'well done' all round.

Off the pitch, David is a smashing lad. On it, he wants to win at all costs. He plays to win, and he's a winner. But, he can be over-aggressive. I saw him tangle with Gary Bennett of Sunderland on TV, and they both ended up being sent off. I'm sorry, Dave, but I thought you were out of order. You could tell as they were running together for 50 yards that Speedie had it in mind to kick out at Bennett, and as the ball went out of play Speedie did just that. Bennett then grabbed Speedie by the throat and it ended up a nasty incident, with both of them dismissed.

He can also be hot-headed in some of the things he gets up to, such as dropping his shorts in front of the fans at Stamford Bridge. It backfired on him, if you pardon the pun! He ended up being charged by the FA with bringing the game into disrepute, and was found guilty and fined. All right, that wasn't very clever, and I'm sure he regrets it, but over all I believe players like David Speedie are good for the game. I always look forward to playing against him, and his type of player. You know exactly where you stand.

Crystal Palace   Andy Gray, who was re-signed by manager Steve Coppell after a spell with Aston Villa, likes to put his foot in and mix it a little bit. But, generally, they are a hard but fair side.

Derby County   Gareth Williams puts himself about. He doesn't mess about in the tackle, but generally they are a fair team who rely on football first.

Everton   Norman Whiteside was sent off for the first time in his career in the FA Cup replay with Oldham at Goodison Park – I'm shocked that it took him so long! He must be the oldest 24 year old in the history of the game. He was playing in the World Cup Finals at the age of 17, and perhaps the danger for Big Norm is that he has done it all too early. But I'm sure he still has ambitions left and targets within the game to aim for. The biggest problem for Whiteside is that he lacks pace, especially when he is coming back from injury and is short of match practice. It's not dirty tactics, it's simply that he's not quick enough and he is guilty of a late tackle. He has been guilty of some late tackles in Merseyside derby games when the pace is so fast that he cannot even get a touch! But also there are, regrettably, times when he goes over the top. That kind of tackle is despised by professionals, because it is a deliberate attempt to injure an opponent. Having said that, I rate Whiteside as a player. He has excellent control, his touch is first class, which explains precisely why he has achieved so much in a short space of time and is able to make up for his lack of pace.

Luton   They have lost one of their best players in Danny Wilson, a midfield performer I rated one of the best in the business. They have also lost their chief so-called hard man Mick Kennedy. Players have accused him in the past of spitting, but he's never done that in my company. But he certainly does a lot of kicking, and gets himself sent off from time to time. When we played at Luton last season, he couldn't get near the ball, let alone near to any of our players, and he was *taken* off after 10 minutes of the second half.

Manchester City   Peter Reid and I have been involved in some marvellous Merseyside battles in the past. Now, after a spell at QPR, he is at Maine Road, back with his old Everton boss Howard Kendall, but his legs have gone a bit. Yet, that doesn't stop him from having a go and he can still dish out a few crunching tackles. Whenever we have battled it out we have always finished the game with a good solid hand-shake, and we'd go off for a drink. We have become good friends off the field as well as fierce rivals on it, and that's just how it should be. Peter is a fabulous fellow, and before the European Championships I roomed with him on England duty. But, just because we are good mates, that doesn't mean I would make it easy for him when we face each other, despite his age!

Manchester United There is no better exponent of the hard, but scrupulously fair tackle in the modern game than England and Manchester United skipper, Bryan Robson. He goes into the tackle, winning a ball he has no right, sometimes, even to consider winning. And he will come out of the challenge with the ball. But that's why he gets so many injuries, he is often too brave for his own good. While Bryan has suffered so many nasty injuries, he has never wilfully gone out to cripple an opponent. He is the perfect example of a highly motivated professional committed 100 per cent to win the ball, and nine times out of ten he will win it.

Millwall The Docklands club have lost their first division status and also sold their most competitive campaigner Terry Hurlock. He looks like a villain, but he is actually a very good player. His long flowing hair makes him look like a gypsy and they called him 'Warlock' at the Den, but although he can give it in the tackle, he can also take it without moaning. He's another vastly underrated player, although he has been recognized by Bobby Robson and has been on the fringe of the England squad in the past. He's a good player to have on your side and that is why Graeme Souness has taken him to Glasgow Rangers.

Norwich Under manager Dave Stringer, the East Anglian club have been on the fringe of the Championship race for a couple of seasons and all credit to them for relying on footballing skills. Yet, they can be hard, but fair. Generally, they rely on outplaying the opposition, trying more to score goals than stop them.

Nottingham Forest Stuart Pearce, the Forest skipper and left-back, certainly lives up to his nickname 'Psycho'. He can be intimidating at times, and his tackling can be best described as 'ruthless'. I can understand it when Bobby Robson said at the time that he was the best left-back he had at his disposal for the World Cup Finals, and when he said, 'Who would want to play against him?' But it does annoy me that our Swedish international defender Glen Hysen was sent off for two 'nothing' challenges without any malice, when there are occasions that Pearce gets away with a diabolical tackle without any punishment. I know he got a yellow card for a tackle against Kevin Gallagher of Coventry in a televised Littlewoods Cup Semi-Final first leg tie, but I have seen him get away with it.

I clashed with him in the League match at Anfield after we first beat Forest in the FA Cup Semi-Final, when I suspect that Brian Clough's team were seeking revenge. Stuart was far from happy that we also won the League match 1–0 with a penalty close to the end – there were a few words exchanged! I'm sure that Stuart Pearce and Neil Webb were out to make a point and get their revenge. When we are together with England, we're the best of mates, but that all changes when the Cup and the Championship are at stake.

QPR   Simon Barker has become an influential figure in the new Rangers team under manager Don Howe. He can kick a little, obviously trying to make an impression! Sadly, he's recently broken his leg – I wish him a swift recovery.

Sheffield Wednesday   Ron Atkinson signed Carlton Palmer from his former club, West Brom, and he made a major contribution. He is a stylish player but he is also strong in the tackle and he can dish it out all right.

Southampton   Former Liverpool favourite Jimmy Case may be getting on in years, but old 'Jimbo' can still put it about in midfield. But it's funny to see the Saints hard man after a game with his deaf-aid in one ear. He looks anything but a menacing midfield man. Here's a player who doesn't mind dishing it out in the tackle and also verbally, but I suppose you have to shout to get your message across! I swear sometimes he pretends to be deaf! Seriously, 'Jimbo' has been deaf in one ear for some time and it has gradually got worse.

I clashed with 'Jimbo' during our heavy defeat at Southampton last season; losing 4–1 was not very pleasant for us and I was guilty of a clumsy tackle on young Ray Wallace. 'Jimbo' came steaming over to me snarling, 'Leave him alone, he's only a kid.' I stormed back, 'Never mind he's only a kid, he's just scored against us, he's no kid to us.' In fact, Rod Wallace had made a goal as well as scoring one. Just like Norman Whiteside, who played in the World Cup Finals at the age of 17, there's an old football saying 'If you're good enough, your old enough'. I don't regret having a 'dig' at Wallace; he was running us ragged. He didn't do too much more after my tackle, but by then he had helped inflict one of our heaviest defeats for some time. At the end of the day, he had the last laugh.

Tottenham Hotspur   Graham Roberts used to be their hard man, but now I would have to nominate only one man at Spurs, Pat van den Hauwe. Their skipper, Gary Mabbut, is not afraid to go in where it hurts, but Pat is a one-off. Actually, he's not a bad lad off the pitch when you get to know him. But on the pitch something can just snap. He can get wound up, particularly if he is annoyed. As a former Evertonian, I will best remember Pat van den Hauwe for one of his derby match tackles on Craig Johnston. It was enough to dissuade our Aussie colleague from taking any liberties during the rest of the match!

Wimbledon   The club's image has improved since the departure of Vinny Jones. In my view, Vinny Jones has a more intimidating mouth than tackle. When he was at Wimbledon he was the king of the verbals.

Vinny Jones has been given a lot of credit for nullifying my impact in the FA Cup Final, so my comments about him might sound like sour grapes. Not at all: I can take it if an opponent outplays me, but the truth is that Liverpool as a team didn't play well and I take my fair share of the blame for that. It has nothing to do with the fact that Vinny Jones made a neck-high tackle on me in the first five minutes of the Final. I got up and got on with the game; that tackle didn't worry me in the least. He could have made a dozen like it and it wouldn't have deflected me from my job. I'm sure he thought it upset me, but I can assure him that it didn't. It is perfectly true that Wimbledon made it difficult for us, but it annoys me intensely that it has been suggested that Vinny Jones marked me out of the game. I didn't think that Vinny Jones had more than six kicks in the entire Wembley Final! And two of them sent the ball into the stands. That was his only contribution. Unfortunately for us, he had the last laugh because he finished on the winning side. That's our fault, collectively.

Tommy Smith was a genuine hard man in the Liverpool team in his day. I've talked with Tommy and he is scathing in his criticism of the so-called hard men of today. He talks about the likes of Dave Mackay, Johnny Giles and Norman Hunter, and of course Tommy was in the same league. But he feels that the hard men of today are soft in comparison to the real hard men of the past.

It may come as a huge surprise to those who know me by watching me play, but don't really know the real me, that I am actually very upset to be tagged a 'hard man', and my wife Julie is most aggrieved by the description. There are occasions when it actually drives me mad! For a start I don't consider myself as a hatchet man in any shape or form and my disciplinary record confirms it. I have been suspended only once and that's not bad in eleven years, particularly for a player in my role in an era of highly competitive football with a top club where so much is always at stake and opponents are out to make their reputations at our expense. I've only been sent off once, and that was at the outset of my career in the circumstances I have already detailed, but in those early days I was fighting desperately for my first-team place and for my career to take off.

I have gone ten successive seasons now without being suspended. I'm proud of that record. I know Gary Lineker has never been booked in his entire career, and I admire the way he takes so much punishment from defenders, but my position, in the heart of midfield, is far more physical. I've also played in some of the fiercest derby games seen anywhere in the world — the Merseyside derby — and I've actually played for both Everton and Liverpool! I have to bite my lip when I'm described as a hard man by journalists. Sure, I go into the tackle hard, but also fairly, in my view, with the aim of winning the ball. I believe in my ability and feel I am as much a constructive player as a destructive one. It even annoys me to have to defend myself.

I refuse even to discuss it if I'm ever asked the question whether I accept that I am one of the game's hard men. My only answer to these questions is for people to look up the statistics and see for themselves that I have played almost 500 games over more than ten years and I've only been suspended once, in my very first season when I was obviously slightly immature. Then examine more closely all my bookings, and a number of them are for dissent rather than for fouls. I'm not saying I am an angel, but I point to my record to emphasize my conviction that there is far more to my game than the average fan might appreciate.

My wife will tell you I am not the type who brags about himself, as Vinny Jones might do! I'm sure she will also tell you that I am nothing like the image I've got. If you were to ask me to paint a picture of myself I would say I am a caring person, especially caring about my family. Perhaps I was not always like that. When I was a teenager I might have been a bit immature and probably did things I would now regret but in those days I never had the time for other people in the way I do now. In that respect perhaps I am a changed person.

Chapter 9

Referees

I'M SORRY TO SAY THAT referees are very, very inconsistent. There are only a handful of referees in the game today whom I can respect, and that is a shocking state of affairs. I admire George Courtney; he is an excellent referee. He knows exactly how far to go with players and, as professionals, we know precisely where we stand with him.

But where are the other acceptable officials? I certainly don't know. Clive Thomas is synonymous with refereeing as far as the general public are concerned. I never liked him. Not because of his decisions, necessarily, but he thought the game of football revolved around him, he fancied the crowd was there to watch him rather than the actual match. I remember Clive Thomas disallowing a Bryan Hamilton goal for Everton from a corner when the score was 2–2, even though, to this day, I've no idea why it was not a perfectly good goal. The verdict from the referee was handball but I didn't see it, and I don't know anyone inside that ground, apart from Clive Thomas, who did. He certainly loved controversial decisions.

Despite my reputation, which I clearly feel is unjust, I have rarely, if at all, crossed swords with referees. I never back chat a

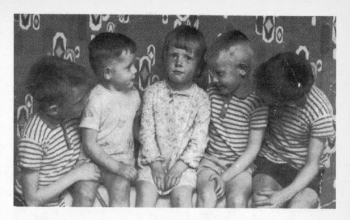

1. With my brothers and sister. I'm on the left, then there's Christopher, Marie, John and Thomas. I'm the second eldest.

2. With the Vernon Colts team which was made up of young players chosen from primary schools in Liverpool. It was while playing with this team that I was noticed by Everton. I'm second from left in the front row.

3. As a ball-boy at Goodison Park I shared the tensions of the team and dreamed of being out on the pitch with them one day. (*Photo: Liverpool Daily Post & Echo Ltd*)

10. In consideration of the observance by the said player of the terms, provisions and conditions of this Agreement, the said _JAMES_ _GREENWOOD_ on behalf of the Club hereby agrees that the said Club shall pay to the said Player the sum of £ _16_ per week from _DECEMBER 19TH 1977_ to _AUGUST 20TH 1978_ and £ _20_ per week from _AUGUST 20TH 1978_ to _AUGUST 20TH 1979_ and £ _____ per week from _____ to _____

and £ _____ per week from _____ to _____ and £ _____ per week from _____ to _____

11. This Agreement (subject to the Rules of The Football Association) shall cease and determine on _AUGUST 20TH 1979_ unless the same shall have been previously determined in accordance with the provisions hereinbefore set forth.

Fill in any other provisions required

WIN BONUSES WILL BE PAID AS UNDER (50% FOR DRAWING GAMES)

RESERVE XI £2.   F.A. YOUTH CUP

'A' 'B' OR ANY   ROUND   2   £1
OTHER YOUTH £1   3   £1.50.
MATCH   4   £2.50.
                        5   £3.50.
          SEMI-FINAL   £4
          FINAL   £6.

As Witness the hands of the said parties the day and year first aforesaid

Signed by the said _JAMES GREENWOOD_ and _STEPHEN McMAHON_

Stephen McMahon
(Player)

In the presence of the Parent or Guardian of the Player

(Signature) _T McMahon_
(Occupation) _UNEMPLOYED_
(Address) _15 BRACKACRE CLOSE_
LIVERPOOL 26

(Secretary)

4. A page of my apprentice player contract with Everton signed on 10th December 1977. The bonuses make interesting reading.

5. The beginning of commercial possibilities during my early days at Everton. A mix of Liverpool and Everton players promote a new car. Standing second from left and receiving the car keys David Johnson, Liverpool, Ray Kennedy, Liverpool, Phil Neal, Liverpool, Mick Lyons, the Everton Captain, and kneeling from left, Peter Eastoe, Everton, and myself.

6. Freddie Starr, centre, a keen Everton supporter with some of the players. I'm on Freddie's right.

7. The Blue Macs: a picture set up by the local paper for the 1980 Everton v. Liverpool match. I'm on the right with Joe McBride of Everton. (*Photo: Tony Kenwright*)

8. Taking the field for the first time as Captain of Everton at Newport.

9. Before kick off at the same match with the mascot, the referee and Wayne Ciegelski of Newport County.

10. The day I signed with Aston Villa. With Villa Manager Tony Barton. (*Photo: Terry Weir*)

11. A portrait taken while I was with Villa.

12. A 'hard-man' clash with Peter Reid of Everton. Jan Molby is on the left. (*Photo: The Mirror Group*)

13. With Kenny Dalglish the day I signed for Liverpool. (*Photo: Barry Farrell Agency*)

14, 15, 16, and *17*. Action
shots taken whilst
playing for Liverpool
and England.
(*14. Associated Sports
Photography – Stewart
Franklin*)
(*15, 16, 17. Associated
Sports Photography –
George Herringshaw*)

18. Hillsborough. The tragedy begins … The man who managed to get onto the pitch had been a neighbour of mine. He told me (in the number 11 shirt) that people were being crushed. (*Photo: Daily Mirror*)

19. The never to be forgotten scenes as floral tributes pour in to Anfield and thousands come to pay their respects. (*Photo: Daily Mirror*)

20. This picture of me was taken by Vicki Hicks a young fan who, along with her sister Sarah, tragically did not survive Hillsborough. The photo was very kindly lent to me by Vicki's parents, Trevor and Jenny Hicks. On the back Vicki had written 'December 14th 1986. Steve McMahon (my favourite player!).' (*Photo: Vicki Hicks*)

21. Making the World Cup record in March 1990. From left, myself, Peter Beardsley, John Barnes and Des Walker. (*Photo: Daily Mirror*)

22. 29th May 1990. Passing the ball to Peter Beardsley in the match against Cagliari in the build up to the World Cup. (*Photo: Daily Mirror*)

23. At home in Liverpool with my wife Julie and the boys, Paul and Stephen.

24. With my World Cup medal.

referee, I rarely show dissent, and that is reflected in my cautions. My attitude is to bite my tongue, count to ten, and walk away from any confrontation with officials. No matter whether you are in the right or not, you can never win an argument with a referee. Irrespective of your point of view, the referee is always right, or at least he thinks he is.

I was booked for the first time in a Merseyside schoolboy match. All I did was to say, 'Jesus Christ'. In the report that followed I was accused and found guilty of using God's name in vain.

I suppose my first formal booking came in the derby FA Youth Cup tie on 5 December 1978. On 13 December I received my first Football Association 'crime' sheet. It was signed by Ted Croker, FA secretary at that time, and sent to the Everton secretary. It read:

Enclosed are two copies of a Caution Report we have received from the Referee of the above match, one copy of which you are required to pass on to the player concerned without delay. The number of penalty points appropriate to the offence is indicated on the Report Form and will be duly recorded against the player.

We would remind you that under the provisions of Item 2 of the current approved disciplinary Procedures, a player who has been cautioned may, within two days of receiving the Referee's Report, send to the Association any observations he may wish to express in relation to the incident, and such observations will be considered by the Disciplinary Committee in the event of the player accumulating 20 or more penalty points within the current Season and thus becoming liable to disciplinary action.

In the Referee's Report I was booked for 'ungentlemanly conduct', and under the heading, 'The incident which came under my notice was as follows', the referee had written in his own hand: 'An opponent had possession of the ball on the wing when S. McMahon deliberately made a late tackle from the side with no intention of playing the ball, fetching his opponent to the ground.'

My first, and last, suspension came in February 1981 as a 19-year-old Everton player. I got a two-match ban for accumulating 20 points after facing a Disciplinary Commission in Manchester. The last of my bookings which took me over the limit was in a Merseyside derby. I missed a fifth round FA Cup tie at Southampton and a League match against Aston Villa at Goodison Park. Manager at that time, Gordon Lee, was quoted as saying:

'It is a pity that the boy has to miss the Cup game but we had a fair hearing. I think it could be because Steve reached 20 points in such a short time that he collected two matches. But that's the way he plays. He's full of enthusiasm and excitement and I don't want him to lose those qualities. The lad will be disappointed, as he will feel he's let the club down. Yet he can learn from his mistakes.'

I can recall I wasn't too happy at the time, and my comments support that view. The *Daily Mirror* quoted me as saying: 'I certainly don't want to come here again. I was hoping I wouldn't get two matches and I'm sick about missing them. The big problem now will be getting back into the side.' I got back into the side, I did learn my lessons – and I never needed to attend another disciplinary hearing. I have never been suspended since.

But my biggest complaint about the standard of refereeing can best be summed up by the experience of my brother John during his days with Everton. He played a reserve game, and during the course of the match made a hefty challenge, a routine tackle as early as the 15th minute.

The referee called him over and said, 'I'm going to book you.' John simply couldn't believe what was happening. 'What's going on?' That was about all he could manage to say to the ref.

What happened next shocked him.

'You're Steve McMahon's brother, aren't you?' said the ref. He went on: 'I've never liked him, so you're getting booked!'

When John told me the story, I was astonished. It seemed so petty. I just wish John had taken the ref's name and reported him to the FA.

It's all very well having a moan, but it's solutions that the game urgently needs to the problem of poor-quality refereeing. The game needs greater consistency, but how that is achieved is the difficulty. I've often heard professional referees put forward as the ideal solution, but it's not mine. I don't agree with the idea, and I certainly wouldn't consider becoming one when I retired from football. I cannot imagine that many ex-professional players would want to become referees.

Nor do I feel that the notion that referees should have a closer relationship with players will make any difference. I don't like the idea of consulting video evidence during the course of a match, as that would turn the game into a circus, akin to some sports in America that stop the action to consult the all-seeing eye in the sky.

More and more TV evidence is being used against players. The TV camera has taken over from the referee, in some serious cases, as the chief arbitrator. Any major incidents missed by the referee, yet caught by the camera, can be used against a player. So why not allow it to be used in favour of a player? If the FA can press charges on the basis of TV evidence, then surely injustices can be overturned with the use of TV evidence. At the moment, players are not allowed to use TV evidence to appeal against a sending off or a booking. That cannot be fair! Even when there has been mistaken identity, there is no right of appeal under the current system of automatic suspensions.

Referees have got to be made aware that one decision can affect a player's livelihood, and it's easy to see why players get so upset. I would like to see younger referees encouraged to come through the ranks and I would like them to be coached by FA coaches to gain knowledge of a player's side of the game.

Chapter 10

Soccer Agents

THE SUBJECT OF SOCCER AGENTS in football is taboo. For a start, they aren't even supposed to exist. Agents are outlawed by FIFA, UEFA, the FA, and the League from being involved in players' transfers, but everyone in the game knows that agents are involved, and the soccer authorities turn a blind eye to them.

There are good agents, there are bad agents. The knack is for a player to find the good ones. A bad agent can be trouble — sometimes serious trouble. One of the best pieces of advice I could pass on to any young professional is to beware soccer agents promising lavish gifts and waving contracts that can earn a player staggering wealth outside the game. I would stipulate not to sign a contract, and be careful of your choice of adviser.

If a player is approached with offers of promotional work and commercial deals from an agent, then he should look at them on their merits, decide on them, and let the agent take his commission. If it works out, then fine, if it doesn't, the player has no long-term commitment. There are some examples of how young players have agreed contracts with agents and signed away 20 per cent of their earnings from their club without realizing what they have done.

Despite the minefield of finding the right agent, it is important to be represented. The game has become big business, and a player, particularly if he progresses up the ladder, will be involved in big-money contracts and transfers. A young lad will need someone he can trust to handle his affairs, either an accountant with some interest in football or a friend who has professional expertise. Ideally, I would like to see the players' union taking more of an active role, and providing young players with a list of approved soccer agents. The PFA are deeply concerned about the roles of agents, and their recommendations would be respected.

Jon Smith of The First Artist Corporation looks after my off-the-field activities and I am more than pleased with his professionalism and his personal advice. I was introduced to Jon through his involvement with the England team. He surrounds himself with people who have been involved in the game, such as Steve Wicks and, before him, Paul Mariner. He looks after the commercial affairs of the England players, orchestrating their World Cup perks pool. He also handles such leading people in the game as Kenny Dalglish, the British record signing of Gary Pallister at £2.3 million, as well as £2 million striker, Tony Cottee, and Aston Villa Players' Player-of-the-Year, David Platt. Others on his books are £1 million striker Roy Wegerle, Chelsea pair Gordon Durie and Steve Clarke, plus Roy Aitken. He is even the UK agent for Argentinian World Cup captain, Diego Maradona, as well as handling the affairs of Ossie Ardiles. His credentials are sound, and he has proved to be a great asset to me.

But Jon is my third agent! The first was Bev Walker. I was introduced to him early in my career, but fortunately I never signed a contract. He was brimming full of things he was going to do for me, but he never produced. There were promises of a sponsored car and more besides, but it was all pie-in-the-sky stuff. That is typical of agents and, for a young kid just coming into the game, it is easy for his head to be turned. I was involved with Bev Walker on and off for a couple of years, before changing.

Next came Eric Hall. I wasn't introduced to him – he introduced himself to me! Liverpool had reached the FA Cup Final and Eric Hall had won the concession to run the players' perks pool. His catch phrase is 'monster, monster busy . . .'. That is part of his answer-phone message. He tends to concentrate on paid articles from national newspapers. Because of the circulation war at the popular end of the newspaper market, players and managers are offered around £1,000 a time for putting their name to an article which is ghost written for them. That was not my style.

Mike Langley of the *Sunday People* wrote in his column that being picked for England had gone to my head because I had started demanding fees before I would agree to any interviews. Well, that was a complete distortion of what actually happened. There was a lot of hype about my selection and there were journalists pestering me on the phone and even coming around to the house for interviews. I got in touch with Eric and asked him to intercept all enquiries and make sure that no one was allowed to come to the house, or continually ringing me up. It seems that there was a misunderstanding between Eric and a few of the pressmen.

As far as I was concerned, the article was inaccurate. Whether it was the newspaper's fault or Eric's did not really bother me. When I picked up the paper the first morning I was with the England party in the team hotel, I was furious. It was the last thing I wanted at such a time. I immediately rang Eric for an explanation. He denied that he had asked newspapers for any money and said, 'There must have been some sort of mix-up.' I told him that the article made me out to be a money grabber and that was not true, and that people tend to believe what they read in the press. I was embarrassed.

I also contacted Mike Langley after my stint of England duty and he said he was sure of his facts and that papers had been asked for large sums of money before I would agree to any interviews. I suppose I could have taken the easy option and blamed the newspaper and kept the man who was promising to make me money out of these types of deals. But I blamed Eric. He was supposed to be looking after my affairs, protecting my image. That was not the kind of way I wanted to make some petty cash on the side. I could have taken the matter further, but I opted not to. But I didn't have anything more to do with Eric Hall.

After a couple of times as part of the England squad, I found Jon Smith to be a genuine man and, after a couple of conversations, agreed to let him represent me. He has been first rate, he doesn't take liberties, he's not out to sting you or anyone else. He doesn't believe in ripping off a few newspapers for a thousand pounds a time, but would rather concentrate on more worthwhile, long-term deals. He never pressurizes me into anything I'm not entirely happy with just to earn a few quid. I even consulted Jon after Hillsborough, when I wanted to get a few things off my chest, but I wanted it done in the right way.

Jon advised me throughout my prolonged negotiations with Liverpool on my new six-year contract. The system at Anfield is that the manager, Kenny Dalgish, informs the club of players he wants to retain on long-term contracts, and then leaves it to the Chief executive, Peter Robinson, to finalize the details of the deal. The club's policy is not to negotiate with agents. Liverpool preferred to meet with me on my own at the club. But they were, of course, fully aware that Jon was behind the scenes influencing my decision.

It made it all a little bit of a farce, because I went out from my talks with the club to telephone Jon to consult with him, and the club knew what I was doing. There must have been four or five meetings with Peter Robinson before the deal was virtually completed. I had a preconceived idea of what I wanted, with the help of Jon, and there was a point when I thought the club would not accept it.

In fact, it became very frustrating. It was a big decision, a very important one on both sides. It was imperative that I had a contract that I was happy with, particularly such a long-term one. At one stage, it was reported that I was unhappy and that I might leave. Well, it never came to that. I'm not saying I wasn't happy, I just wanted to get it all sorted out amicably, and eventually it was.

But there was a great deal of Press. I was linked with Sampdoria, Bordeaux, Napoli and Torino. Sampdoria President, Paulo Mantovani, was reported to have bid £2.5 million and, according to a *Sunday Mirror* report on 2 July 1989, as saying: 'We are determined to get him – he's my kind of player.' There was even speculation that the Genoa club were prepared to make an initial down payment of around £100,000 to secure first option. *The Times* confirmed that a bid had been made, but had been rejected out of hand by Liverpool.

A lot of agents would have actively pursued the opportunity of being involved in a big-money move to the Continent. That is a way of making a financial killing. There is always a big slice of the action there for an agent. But, to his credit, Jon never once tried to nudge me to go to Sampdoria. He left the decision to me. And I chose to commit myself to Liverpool for the rest of my playing career. However, I would not be telling the truth if I didn't admit to being interested in the fact that Sampdoria wanted to sign me. I asked Liverpool if the Italian club had been in touch. They were quite open with me, and told me that they had, but they had declined immediately. The Italians were told 'no chance'. It was flattering all round, and I was impressed by Liverpool's frankness. Of course, I was tempted. Any player would be. But the decision was not mine to make. There was a year left of my contract and that decision rested with Liverpool. Yes, I would have left had it been right for Liverpool, because I've no doubt if they had thought it was a deal in their best interests they would have taken it.

Before I finally signed the six-year contract, I arranged a meeting with Jon to go through all the finer points of the deal. Once the contract was signed, my mind was put at ease, and my future secured – without having to go abroad.

Chapter 11

Dressing-room Humour

SOMETIMES FOOTBALL TAKES ITSELF too seriously. I know Bill Shankly once said that football isn't life or death, it's more important – and I know what he means. The game is big business, there is so much at stake, perhaps too much, but the old values of sportsmanship, dressing-room humour and comradeship aren't things of the past as so many people would have you believe.

I'd like to take you into the Liverpool dressing-room, and behind the scenes at Anfield to highlight the fun side of the game, and appreciate that professional footballers like to laugh and joke rather than the popular image of men out to win-at-all-costs, to grasp as many of the rewards that are going.

Our eccentric goalkeeper, Bruce Grobbelaar, is one of the funniest men I've ever met. He tells a funny story and I hope he'll forgive me for revealing it. I hope he doesn't take offence – because he can sometimes become quite aggressive!

Bruce used to be a jungle fighter in his Army days in Zimbabwe and he relates this story about how he and his mate were making their way through the jungle when they were confronted by a cobra. Well, how do you handle a cobra? Bruce would say, 'Quite easy, really', and, dead pan, he would go on to explain, 'All you do is to wave your fingers a few inches in front of its face and, while you've attracted its attention, smack it in the back of the head with your other hand . . . skin it, then eat it!'

Of course, Bruce is being perfectly serious about it all, but we're all rolling about.

'What does it taste like?' one of the lads would ask Bruce.

'It's a bit like chicken, but more tender!' No one believes him for one minute. Can you imagine standing a couple of feet from a cobra, waving your fingers in its face while smacking it in the back of the head – you'd run a mile.

Steve Nicol looks a dour sort of bloke, but nothing could be further from the truth. Steve is a crisp and cola addict, and he loves junk food. If he is ever a bit sluggish in training the lads rib him about eating a dozen packets of crisps and downing six bottles of Coke the night before. Steve is a lovely fellow but sometimes can be just a little bit gullible. The lads love a practical joke, and Steve has suffered more than once at the hands of the Anfield dressing-room pranksters.

I've been told a couple of tales about Steve that occurred before I arrived at Anfield. It was in the days that Graeme Souness and Kenny Dalglish were together as players. Along with Steve, the trio were on their way to team up with the Scottish international squad. They were in Graeme's car with Steve in the back, and the conditions were atrocious with heavy snow falling. Graeme and Kenny decided to wind up Steve. Graeme stopped the car and told Steve to get out to wipe the snow from the back window. Steve, dressed only in a T-shirt, nipped out of the back and, as he was about to wipe off the snow, Graeme drove off! They turned up half an hour later, by which time poor Steve was virtually frozen solid. To many people that might not seem to be a very clever thing to do, but that is typical of Graeme Souness–Kenny Dalglish humour.

In fact, it gets worse. The team were away in Israel and the lads went out for a few beers in the afternoon. Kenny went back to the hotel as he likes to rest or get some sleep. But Steve was not aware of his routine and asked Alan Hansen why Kenny had gone to his room. 'You don't know about Kenny!'

And, of course, Steve didn't know. 'What do you mean?' said Steve.

Alan said: 'He's got leukaemia.'

'Go away,' said Steve, 'who are you kidding?'

Alan added, 'But that's why he goes to bed, Steve.'

Steve then said, 'I thought there might be something wrong when he seemed to get so much pain in his shoulder when he brought the ball down in our last match.'

Alan replied, 'That's right, I remember that.'

Steve went on, 'I wondered why Kenny has been so depressed lately, it's terrible. Now I know why he likes to be alone so much. I think I'll go and see him.'

As Steve went up in the lift, Ronnie Whelan quickly phoned Kenny's room and filled him in on the joke. There was a knock on Kenny's door. Kenny got into bed. 'Come in,' said Kenny.

As soon as Steve got through the door he immediately said, 'Are you all right, Kenny?'

'Yes, I'm all right, no problem,' said Kenny.

'I'm sorry to hear about it,' said Steve.

'Don't worry,' said Kenny, 'it's just one of those things.'

At this point the other lads had crept upstairs, and, of course, Kenny had left his door unlocked. Steve went on, 'I knew there was something wrong that day when you were in so much pain.'

Kenny couldn't contain himself much longer, he was virtually in tears trying to contain the laughter, but finally the giggles burst out and the other lads burst into the room. Only Nico would fall for such a line.

That should have been enough to warn Steve about the antics of Souness and Dalglish – but it didn't. The pair of them cooked up another plot when they told Steve they had set him up with a lucrative boots deal. They told Steve to turn up to meet the man from sportswear company Puma at 1 p.m. on a Sunday at the Burtonwood Service Station off the M62 and he would have the money for him. He took his wife Eleanor along and after a four-hour wait she told him, 'I told you, Steve, they're all winding you up.'

Graeme and Kenny never thought for one minute that Steve would go along to the motorway service station, but when Steve turned up for training the next morning Graeme asked, 'Did you turn up to see that fellow?'

Steve replied, 'Don't be silly, I knew you were winding me up!' It took him three weeks to admit that he did turn up and that he felt such a fool.

Well, twice bitten, but not Steve. He fell for it a third time when the boys invited him and his missus to a men's only function. Poor Eleanor was the only wife to turn up. She went along all dressed up only to have to go home!

It might all sound cruel, but it's all part of the fun that goes on, and no one really takes offence. I should know because I've not escaped. I have also been on the receiving end of an embarrassing escapade from the Joke Department.

Page Three girl Kathy Lloyd appeared in the newspaper one day, in one of her more familiar poses, and the caption said that the Liverpool player she most fancied was yours truly. Well, you can imagine the stick I took that day. It started the minute I got to the training ground that morning. I discovered that Kenny Dalglish had pinned the picture and the article to the dressing-room notice-board. Kenny then hatched a little scheme with Roy Evans, and, of course, it was kept from me. My wife Julie told me later that she had received a telephone call at home from a *News of the World* reporter while I was at training. 'We have seen the article where Kathy Lloyd fancies Steve McMahon. We would like to arrange a picture of Kathy and Steve together – we were thinking perhaps of Steve in his shorts and Kathy topless, that would be nice.'

Julie replied, 'I don't think Steve will do that.'

Julie told me that she was going mad but desperately trying to control her anger and keep calm on the phone.

The 'reporter' didn't give up easily and went on, 'Oh, I'm sure Steve won't mind, and we will pay him well.'

Julie went on, 'Look, it's got nothing to do with me, I'll ask Steve when he comes home.'

But Julie couldn't wait. She rang me up at Anfield. 'Has anyone been on from the *News of the World* asking you to pose for a picture with Kathy Lloyd?'

'Don't be daft,' I said, 'it will be one of the lads or The Gaffer.' The bogus reporter was actually Roy Evans.

Ronnie Whelan and his wife Elaine are very close friends of Julie and myself. The night after our Cup Final victory which clinched the Double in 1986, everybody had loads to drink at the celebration banquet, in a London hotel, as one might expect. It was rather late but we were still in party mood and looking for Ronnie and Elaine to join us. We asked where they had got to and were told that they had gone up to their room. We went up there and found Ronnie and Elaine in bed. We sent down for some more bottles of champagne. As we were relaxing, Julie took off her party dress and slipped into a towel and dressing-gown she found in the bathroom. Julie was sitting on the edge of the bed when there was a knock on the door and in came the waiter with the champagne. He had an expression on his face as if to say 'What the hell is going on in here?'. He must have thought there was some sort of orgy going on as I was the only one dressed. Julie was embarrassed and trying to bury her head in the bed so as not to be recognized, but Ronnie didn't seem to mind having two undressed women in his room!

Ronnie relates a fascinating true story that provides a perfect insight into the total dedication and single-mindedness of Bob Paisley. Ronnie says he was in the treatment room when a conversation took place between Paisley, the then physiotherapist, and one of the young Liverpool apprentices. Bob was giving the youngster treatment on his injured knee. The lad asked Bob, 'What should I do when I get home to speed up the recovery because the knee kills me when I walk upstairs?'

Paisley replied, 'Tell your dad to sell the house and buy a bungalow.'

The biggest comic in the England World Cup squad is, of course, Paul Gascoigne, the player whom Bobby Robson once described as 'daft as a brush' and the next day at Bisham Abbey, the England training headquarters, the Spurs player ran out with a brush sticking out of his sock!

Everyone has their favourite Gazza story. The one I like best came about the time that Bobby Robson was suffering a mauling from the media, and was under an enormous amount of pressure, with a section of Fleet Street calling for the manager's head. During a practice game on the training pitch, Gazza suddenly leapt on the manager's back! No one could believe it. Gazza climbed on to Robson's back and shouted 'Never mind, boss, get your head up.' It certainly made us all laugh, and brought a smile back to the face of Bobby Robson.

It might seem incredible but Gazza isn't the daftest footballer I've ever come across, nor the funniest. The No. 1 comedian, albeit a purely subjective view, of course, is my former Everton team-mate John Bailey. He is just a scream. What a character.

Before a game we would all stroll out to test the pitch conditions and there would be John wearing one of the most outlandish masks that he had bought at the joke shop. He would be wearing a huge mac. Supporters would be asking themselves, 'Who's that?' There might be 40,000 people in the stadium totally baffled and trying to guess who it was. You can imagine the fans after the match talking about it in the pubs and clubs, still wondering who it was.

Half the time, John wouldn't realize what he was saying and the lads would wind him up. John played once for the England B side and whenever anyone brought the national team or the World Cup into the conversation he would always say how proud he was on the day he wore an England shirt and played for his country. He would go on about the England badge, the national anthem, and no one would have been prouder than him. He said he felt goose pimples all over when the band started to play ... and then he would burst into song – only to hum the tune from the American anthem, but without having a clue that he was doing it. He had been going on for so long about how patriotic he was, but then didn't know our own national anthem! Well, we all fell about. But it wasn't a joke to John, and he couldn't understand why we were all laughing at him, and that only made us roll about even more.

He would always get himself into a tangle because he was such an enthusiastic bloke. He would always get his sayings muddled up. For instance, if he was describing a player he had to mark, he would say, 'He can spin on a five pence piece', when he meant to say, 'He could turn on a sixpence.'

He would tell me a story about Noel Brotherstone, the former Spurs player, who moved on to play on the wing for Blackburn Rovers and Northern Ireland. Now, poor Noel has lost most of his hair, and John swears that he lost it one day after training as he was coming out of Ewood Park when he tripped over and fell on the side of the kerb, and, with his head lying on the kerb, a bus came along and whisked his hair off. You could imagine that the lads at Blackburn had been winding him up and telling him that this was how Noel lost his hair and that John had fallen for their tale. He fell for it so completely that when he told me the story he was serious – it was hilarious!

Chapter 12

World Cup Diary

THE WORLD CUP DRAW in Rome on 9 December 1989 paired England against Jack Charlton's Republic of Ireland, reviving bitter memories of England's disastrous opening European Championship match with the Irish in Stuttgart. It was very much a significant draw for me, as I almost decided to play for the Republic!

After I played for Everton as a 19 year old against Liverpool, at one of my first derby games, Eion Hand, the Republic manager at that time, came to the game to watch me, and he approached me afterwards in the players' lounge. He told me that he was impressed with my performance and wanted me to play for the Irish. My team-mate Eamon O'Keefe was already in the Republic's squad and he introduced me to Eion Hand.

I can't recall how I qualified for the Irish, because I'm a Scouser and proud of it, and only had ambitions to play for England. But the Irish were on the look-out for as many players from the First Division they could find with dual nationality and they traced an Irish link with my grandparents – I think one of them once had an Irish wolf hound as a pet!

Eion Hand asked if I would consider playing for the Irish and I said that I would. A *Sunday People* report in February 1981 stated: 'Sadly, when McMahon early in the season was more inclined towards the Republic, the Irish did not have on schedule the under-21 fixture that could have been used to commit the youngster.'

To be honest, I would have played for the Irish had England not discovered that I might 'defect' to them, and called me up for their under-21 squad. I would probably have waited around a year before deciding to play for the Republic. I never consulted anyone about whether I should take up the Irish offer, but I did give it some thought. However, just three weeks after the first report about the Irish connection appeared in the Press, I was called up for the England under-21 squad. As the *Daily Mirror* reported at the time: 'Steve McMahon is poised to make his international debut tomorrow to cap a "Roy of the Rovers" season for the Everton youngster.' The *Daily Star* put it this way: 'Steve McMahon's meteoric rise to stardom takes another giant step.' My quote at the time was: 'It's been an incredible season. Last summer I'd have laughed at anyone who suggested I'd be a First Division regular, let alone win an under-21 cap.'

Ironically, I was picked by Dave Sexton to play against the Republic of Ireland at Anfield. We won 2–0 and my Everton team-mate Kevin Sheedy was carried off with a damaged ankle.

I am delighted that I came to the right choice. Of course I would have had 60 or more caps had I chosen the Republic of Ireland. By the time my career was over I could have had as many caps as Peter Shilton. But with due respect to the Republic, 12 England caps are worth more than 50 caps with the Irish.

At Anfield we have several Republic of Ireland internationals, including Steve Staunton and Ronnie Whelan. Ray Houghton plays for the Irish but he has Scottish parentage, and is as Cockney as they come. I suppose he's something of a mongrel!

My England breakthrough came in Tel Aviv on 18 February 1988. It's an old footballing saying that you make your own luck in this game, and that is true in as much as I had to be playing at the top of my form to justify my selection against Israel, but I had to rely on the withdrawals of Peter Reid and Glenn Hoddle, and then skipper Bryan Robson was ruled out. But as I said at the time:

> 'I felt sorry for Bryan. But someone's disappointment is another's joy and that is the case for me. It was funny . . . I said to Bryan, "How are you?" when I met him in the corridor after training. Tongue in cheek he said, "Don't worry, you'll be playing." I'm absolutely delighted because it's been my lifetime's ambition to play for my country. When I rang my wife Julie to break the news she asked me twice if I was joking. She didn't think I was being serious.'

Bobby Robson commented at that time: 'Steve has improved this season, he's been running the midfield at Liverpool. Barnes and Beardsley have been outstanding, but in the early part of the season McMahon and Ronnie Whelan were superb. Arguably, Steve was the best player when I saw them against Aston Villa.'

I made my debut in one of the youngest and least experienced England line-ups under Robson, the entire team had just 105 caps between them: Chris Woods (Glasgow Rangers), Gary Stevens (Everton), Dave Watson (Everton), Mark Wright (Derby County), Stuart Pearce (Nottingham Forest), Chris Waddle (Spurs), Steve McMahon (Liverpool), Neil Webb (Nottingham Forest), John Barnes (Liverpool), Clive Allen (Spurs), Peter Beardsley (Liverpool). I remember at the time thanking my dad, Peter Beardsley, John Barnes and Colin Harvey for such an important landmark in my career. The national papers quoted me as saying:

'The England manager comes to watch our games a lot because of Peter and John and that must have helped me personally to catch his eye. While they have quite rightly earned all the headlines, I'd like to think I've been consistent, and that's important. I've certainly improved this season. At Anfield there are that many players, you are doing well just to be in the team.'

On the flight home from Tel Aviv, with Peter Beardsley leading the celebrations for Robson's 55th birthday in the absence of Bryan Robson, my chances of making the European Championship squad had dramatically come to light because of my performance against Israel. The *Daily Mirror*'s assessment of it was: 'Clearly McMahon's spirited display was one of the major pluses in an otherwise dreadful match in atrocious conditions.' The England manager was quoted as saying: 'I have learned quite a bit from certain performances. McMahon could have had a harder debut, not in terms of conditions, but the opposition. But it is obvious he could go into my squad. He is fighting for a place in midfield with several others and he would not look out of place. The way he adapted to meet the conditions proves he would be a very useful player.'

Neil Webb returned for the next game against Holland but then I played against Hungary in the Nep Stadium in Budapest at the end of April 1988 – alongside Bryan Robson. It's amusing to look back at what I said at the time:

'It will make a nice change from kicking each other for 90 minutes! Robbo and I want to win so badly – we have had some fearsome battles against each other in Liverpool–Manchester United clashes. But we get on well. I respect him and learn from him, and it's absolutely brilliant to get this chance to play alongside him. This is a great chance to show that I really am good enough for my country.'

The team was: Chris Woods (Glasgow Rangers), Viv Anderson (Manchester United), Gary Pallister (Middlesbrough), Tony Adams (Arsenal), Stuart Pearce (Nottingham Forest), Gary Stevens (Everton), Bryan Robson (Manchester United), Steve McMahon (Liverpool), Chris Waddle (Spurs), Gary Lineker (Barcelona), Peter Beardsley (Liverpool). The England manager was quoted as saying: 'The time was right to have another look at McMahon. Someone had to go out and Webb has looked a little stale lately.'

It was a depressing end to the season, failing to clinch the Double by losing to Wimbledon in the FA Cup Final but, at least, I was delighted to clinch a place in the European Championship squad. The first choice midfield pairing was Bryan Robson and Neil Webb for the opening game with the Republic of Ireland, with Glen Hoddle coming on as a substitute on the hour and then starting the second match against Holland, while I played in the final game against Russia when England's fate had already been sealed.

The team for my one appearance in West Germany was: Chris Woods (Glasgow Rangers), Gary Stevens (Everton), Dave Watson (Everton), Tony Adams (Arsenal), Kenny Sansom (Arsenal), Trevor Steven (Everton), Bryan Robson (Manchester United), Steve McMahon (Liverpool), John Barnes (Liverpool), Glenn Hoddle (Monaco), Gary Lineker (Barcelona). I was substituted after 54 minutes with Neil Webb coming on, while Gary Lineker went off after 69 minutes with Mark Hateley coming on in a bitterly disappointing 3–1 defeat and England finishing bottom of the group without a single point, seven goals against and only two scored.

After such a set-back for the footballing nation, there was so much determination among the players to fight to win back their pride and convince a doubting public. Qualification for the World Cup achieved just that. England were on the road to Italy . . .

Monday 22 January   England had a two-day get-together at Lillishall. Bobby Robson wanted all of his players to undergo thorough physiological tests. The idea is that any player who is injured can measure his recovery rate against the 'score' he makes in these tests. Because it was the week building up to our live TV match in the FA Cup at Norwich, the Liverpool players were not subjected to the full rigours of the tests. Instead, I had to suffer no more than a pin prick, as I had a blood test. I eventually underwent the full-scale stamina tests when I joined up for the Brazil match, taking them on the extensive lawn outside our team headquarters at the Burnham Beeches Hotel.

Sunday 25 March   The normal routine under Bobby Robson is to report at our hotel headquarters at 7 p.m. A light meal is available and the players sit down together. The manager and his back-room staff ensure that everyone has arrived and assess the injuries, with the manager making check calls and deciding whether to call up replacements.

The England players are paired up to share rooms; the company helps to pass some of the more monotonous periods of the time away from home. I'm usually the odd man out! That's because my Liverpool team-mates John Barnes and Peter Beardsley room together, leaving me to sort something out with one of the other lads. On this occasion I roomed with Chelsea's talented Australian-born left-back Tony Dorigo, understudy to first choice Stuart Pearce.

The reason I paired up with Tony is simply that we knew each other from our Aston Villa days together. Tony was on a 'high'

120

after scoring the winner for Chelsea against Middlesbrough and was kept busy from the moment he arrived with a succession of interviews for Australian radio. Tony is a smashing bloke, laid-back, quiet, and a lover of golf. I enjoy a round or two myself, but I'm not in Tony's league.

Monday 26 March Once again, it is custom and practice for Mondays to consist of a light training session at nearby Bisham Abbey. The facilities there are superb, the playing surface excellent. A coach transports the players to the training sesssion and we return to the hotel to change and have lunch. A number of players will miss this session because of knocks at the weekend matches.

As it was getting close to the departure date for Italy and because the Brazil match was the biggest of the final World Cup warm-up matches at Wembley, the team's agent Jon Smith of First Artist Corporation was kept busy with a number of commercial schemes. The players' priority is to seek the glory for themselves and for their country in Italy, but we are all professionals and the players' pool is a normal part of the build-up. In fact, it does have the beneficial effect of keeping the players' minds occupied. A coach took us from our hotel to the Top Man store in Oxford Street. Top Man are one of the players' main World Cup sponsors. The store was shut at 6.30 p.m. but the staff remained on duty, the media were invited, and the players were given cash vouchers to roam the place and take their choice of the merchandise. All the players who turned out for the publicity pictures were given £500 worth of vouchers as part of Top Man's endorsement of the England World Cup squad. Of course, I'm the one who ends up getting the bad publicity with a picture of me with the caption saying I needed three assistants to handle all my new gear . . . it was actually four!

Tuesday 27 March Once again, the training is light. There is little point in exhausting the international players who have been training extensively and playing all season with their clubs. The manager names his team on the training pitch before this session, and then goes through set pieces and set plays. Even though it was expected that I would be chosen, it was still a big thrill to be playing against Brazil. England skipper Bryan Robson was missing, as he was recuperating following a hernia operation, and Neil Webb was still on his come-back programme after rupturing an Achilles tendon during the World Cup qualifying tie in Stockholm against Sweden in September. This was a big opportunity for me to stake a claim for a place in the starting line-up against the Republic in Cagliari on 11 June, a vital date for English football. With so much competition for places, particularly in midfield, it felt as if the manager had a lot of faith in me.

Back at the hotel the manager held a team meeting. He wanted us to put certain dates in our diaries concerning the Denmark and Uruguay games and then the departure date for the World Cup. Bobby Robson gave us a choice: we could either remain in our hotel after the Denmark game or return to our families for just a couple of days before reassembling for the Uruguay match. Because we are away from home for five weeks we voted to return home, albeit for just two days. We were all grateful to the manager for taking such a democratic decision. He could have insisted that we remained in the hotel.

Wednesday 28 March The morning of the match means another stint on the training pitch, again a light session, concentrating on set pieces such as corners, and free kicks. My role when the opposition are attacking at corners is to guard the area outside the box, to block any attempted shots or to challenge for knock downs. When we are on the offensive my role is again to patrol the perimeter of the penalty area, seeking shooting chances or just to gain possession.

After a light meal, we travel to Wembley and prepare for one of the biggest games any professional is ever likely to encounter, against the South American stars, wondering if we shall confront them when it matters even more, in the World Cup Finals.

You never really like praising yourself, but I must admit I was pleased with my performance and that of the England team's against the Brazilians. It is not often England beats Brazil, so this was an occasion to savour and remember. It was also a huge morale boost for the entire England squad, and perhaps an indication of our chances in Italy. I felt this was a very important game in front of a packed Wembley stadium, with 80,000 fans witnessing the improvements the England team has shown over the past eighteen months to two years.

Let's face it, you don't really expect to accomplish too many attacking moves against Brazil; the object is to stop them playing and hit them on the break, and this we did very successfully. The England team is very strong at set pieces and we anticipated exploiting this advantage, which we did.

It was a vital match from my point of view. I wanted to emphasize to the England manager that if our skipper Bryan Robson is injured, I can fill his boots. I have enough confidence in my own ability to believe that I have done enough to deserve a place in the side, but I am also a realist. With all his players at his disposal and fully fit, I would expect the England manager to select Bryan Robson and Neil Webb in the centre of midfield, and his previous team selections when they have both been available have illustrated that. Webbie has recovered from his Achilles injury with remarkable speed, and my feeling was that I was battling with Webbie for a place in the team.

It was a bitter-sweet ending for me because the enjoyment of beating Brazil was soured by their surprising lack of sportsmanship. They clearly did not like losing to us at Wembley so close to the World Cup Finals. I offered my hand in friendship after the game, a traditional thing in football, but hardly any of their players shook hands.

Normally, in international football, opponents are more than willing to swap shirts with us. Now, I regard my England shirt as precious, but I was willing to give it up in return for a coveted Brazil shirt. I was among a number of England players who asked Fred Street and Norman Medhurst to nip into the Brazil dressing-room and offer to swap shirts. But the Brazil trainer returned to our dressing-room with their training kit! The shirts had stick-on badges. It was an insult. My attitude was 'stuff you' and keep your training kit, you're not having my England shirt in exchange for that. I was disappointed, to say the least.

Sunday 22 April The England squad assembled at The Queens Hotel, City Square, West Yorkshire by 5 p.m. to attend the Royal Variety Club Dinner, a World Cup send-off in our honour. It was a great evening, a marvellous way to relax listening to the jokes of Frank Carson and Bob 'The Cat' Bevan. We helped to raise £95,000 for a worthy cause.

Monday 23 April We departed the Queens Hotel for Burnham Beeches. Because of the amount of travelling, the only extra exertion was an hour's light training session on the hotel lawn, after which Bobby Robson held a Press conference. My room-mate for this international was Steve Hodge. Steve likes to mix a lot with his pals from Forest and so I hardly saw him. Most of the time I ended up in my room on my own, but that's no problem as Gazza is always popping in to keep me amused!

Gazza just cannot keep still and he cannot sit down and relax. If you want an afternoon's sleep after a training session, you've got no chance with Gazza on the prowl. Once you've nodded off, Gazza's on the phone shouting down the line before hanging up! But Gazza is the life and soul of the party and we all want him to go to Italy and we'll all be sick if he doesn't make it. He'll be great for team spirit. He's so funny with his little games and pranks.

Gazza took an awful lot of stick leading up to this match, which was obviously going to be so important to him and he took it to heart. He doesn't like the Press. In fact, he hates them. He feels they have built him up just to knock him down. He didn't actually say an awful lot but I can imagine that the *Daily Mirror*'s pictures of him on the morning of the match dressed up as a clown would have got to him. All he said was, 'Have you seen these pictures here?' The normal punter would have thought that the pictures were taken on the day before the match, when in reality he posed for them for a Christmas annual. That sort of thing is bound to have an effect on a young lad; let's face it, I would have been annoyed if I had been in his shoes. Then, again, you cannot blame the newspaper for publishing pictures the lad quite happily posed for. I wouldn't have posed like that in the first place, and that's a lesson for him to learn. You have got to expect those kind of pictures to be used again, and again.

Tuesday 24 April   It came as absolutely no surprise that the England manager chose Paul Gascoigne. The speculation has been non-stop that Gazza would play against Czechoslovakia. I was very disappointed to be left out, but I had no complaints as Gazza needed his chance and deserved it. With Bryan Robson back in the international fold for the first time since his hernia operation, there was no room for me.

Wednesday 25 April   Gazza made three goals, two for Steve Bull, and scored a breath-taking goal himself in a 4–2 win. You cannot take it away from him, he did excellently, and I was pleased for him. After all the pressure, all the pre-match hype, he responded well. However, no one can really judge him on one game, and his performance warrants another crack in the side. The Czechs were not Brazil! Of course I will be disappointed again if I'm left out against Denmark in the next World Cup build-up match, but once again I've got to be a realist and Gazza has got to be given another go to see what he's made of.

The crunch match on the horizon is the Uruguay game. Bobby Robson has already indicated that he wants to play his prospective World Cup starting formation, so it's no surprise that everyone desperately wants to be selected for that one. Even so, a lot can happen between that game and the start of the World Cup in Cagliari. All I can do is to keep my fingers crossed and hope.

After Gazza's performance there was a great deal of debate about England's best formation, the ideal system, but it's my view that an England team, playing in the heat of Sardinia, cannot afford three out-and-out attacking midfield players in Bryan Robson, Chris Waddle and Paul Gascoigne. That will leave us a little wide open. Perhaps the manager can take such a risk in certain games, but they would have to be carefully selected matches. My guess is that the squad system will be vital in temperatures of 90 degrees, and that substitutes will play an increasingly important role. Equally, it can be a dangerous game, as Sir Alf Ramsey discovered in Mexico in 1970 when he substituted Bobby Charlton and Martin Peters when England were strolling towards the Quarter-Finals against West Germany, and ended up going out.

At this distance it is difficult to make predictions about the World Cup, but I believe that England will surprise a lot of people – even our own manager! Sometimes I'm not really sure that he believes we are capable of doing very well. We are very strong in the air and at set pieces, and that's where we will be dangerous. Defensively, there are not many better-equipped teams in the world, and we can also be creative; Gary Lineker can always score goals, and there are plenty of other players dotted around the team with goal capabilities.

In fact, I'd go as far as to say that I feel that we have a great chance of actually winning it. Now wouldn't that be something? My favourites, alongside England, would be Italy, Brazil, and West Germany. Yet, we've played both Italy and Brazil and come out of both games with a lot of credit. I see no reason to fear any team in the Finals.

Chapter 13

World Cup Diary:
Bobby Robson Fiasco

No ONE COULD POSSIBLY HAVE imagined that England's World Cup send-off to Cagliari would have been so controversial: manager Bobby Robson's departure after eight years in charge was prematurely and messily leaked, and Paul Gascoigne was involved in a punch-up outside a Newcastle bar.

The countdown to Cagliari really got under way with the final two warm-up matches at Wembley and the announcement of the World Cup squad. The tension and anticipation were beginning to mount.

Monday 14 May With Bryan Robson and Neil Webb unavailable because of their involvement in the FA Cup Final replay, I was chosen as Paul Gascoigne's 'minder' for the match with Denmark. Of course, I was delighted to be playing for England, as I am every time I represent my country, but I have to admit that my mission was not one that I relished.

My instructions from Bobby Robson were to sit in the 'hole', that is the area behind Gazza in midfield, and protect him, to allow him to express himself and make attacking surges. I was told not to get carried away and feel the urge to go forward myself. Now, that is not my game at all. It was all very well for

Gazza — it suited him fine and was designed to cover up his defensive deficiencies while concentrating on his strengths — but even at the time I felt that it restricted me. Selfish, maybe, but surely I was entitled to try to impress for my own good, as I wanted to play for England in the World Cup, and I wanted to produce my best form to stake my claims in the eyes of the England manager. Instead, I helped Gazza stake his own claims because I adhered to the manager's orders without quibbling, without the slightest moan. (When I look back on the World Cup, I cannot help but have feelings of resentment that I spent the pre-tournament build-up aiding Gazza while my own chances were diminishing. I suppose they are natural feelings of frustration, but in no way do I begrudge Gazza his opportunity, which of course he took in spectacular fashion.)

Tuesday 15 May　The match itself was average, hardly inspiring with the World Cup so close, but it was important for Gazza to have a successful game after the euphoria of his performance against the Czechs. From that viewpoint, the match was worth while. So, on a personal level, under the circumstances, it went quite well for me. The Danes looked quite useful in the first half but Gary Lineker scored in the second half, enabling us to stretch our unbeaten run to 17 matches.

Friday 18 May　After a couple of days' break at home, the squad reassembled at the hotel. Manchester United won the FA Cup Final replay, and Bryan Robson and Neil Webb were able to join up, although they didn't arrive until the Sunday.

Monday 21 May　The big day had arrived — the manager announced his World Cup squad of 22. Personally, I felt confident that I could be included, but you never know for sure until the squad is actually named. The manager never told anyone privately that they were going, and that even included the most senior players like skipper Bryan Robson and keeper Peter

Shilton. There were question marks against some players and they knew it. There had been a great deal of speculation in the Press, and the players were aware that it was informed speculation, as the manager had a habit of giving a little bit of information away in certain quarters. The squad had virtually been picked beforehand in the Press, and for some players that probably made it even worse. I am sure they would have preferred to have been informed by the manager himself rather than have to read about it before being officially told. For that reason, it was not such a big shock when the announcement finally arrived. None the less, it was tough to take for those left out.

After training, we returned by coach to the team hotel and, outside on the lawn in the midday sunshine, Bobby Robson assembled the players to read out the list of the privileged 22 players who would proudly represent England in the World Cup. When everybody stood up I could see the disappointment in the eyes of David Rocastle. He felt he should have been going, but he had read that he was going to be one of those to be disappointed. Those players not selected were given the option by the manager to stay on and attend the final match before departure. I can imagine that their view must have been 'what's the point?'. David Rocastle decided to go home to the comfort of his family and he did so with the manager's consent and knowledge. Naturally, the decision was a body blow and anyone in his position would be terribly down-hearted, but he took it like a man. There was no complaint.

There was some surprise over the inclusion of Mark Wright because he had been suffering from a badly bruised thigh. The manager had pointed out that he had not received treatment for a week because the season had ended and that the internal bleeding had not cleared. Mark was unable to train and certainly couldn't play. It was causing him a major problem. Mark's place in the squad was in doubt right up until the last minute, with Arsenal captain Tony Adams standing by.

Tuesday 22 May   Bryan Robson was restored to the centre of midfield against Uruguay. I was back on the bench and never got on. But the strategy of allowing Gazza the midfield freedom with the 'second' midfield player in the 'hole' was retained. Bryan is at his most devastating with the freedom to go on attacking sortees whenever he wants. He can pop up inside the box and score vital goals as he has proved so often in the past. Whenever he played alongside Gazza he seemed to have a very, very quiet game. Just like myself, Bryan found himself restricted. In my view, the England manager had not been able to devise a system to get the best out of Bryan Robson or whoever played alongside the Spurs midfield player.

That was not the only problem Bobby Robson seemed incapable of solving. Of course, it is only my opinion and the game is all about opinions, so I cannot see any objections to expressing my personal view that Bobby Robson did not know his best line-up, even though he professed that he did.

He could not come to grips with the enigma of John Barnes. At Anfield he was inspirational for a Liverpool team in which I knew from first-hand experience exactly how well he functioned. Robson tried him wide, up front alongside Gary Lineker, in a free role behind the main striker. But, in whichever role or position he played, he failed to reproduce the sort of exciting skills that deservedly earned him the winning votes from the country's football writers as Footballer of the Year. The England manager wanted to stick with his tried and trusted 4–4–2 formation but was undecided whether to play John Barnes and Chris Waddle as the wide pair, or introduce Trevor Steven and play Barnes through the middle.

The other problem revolved around Peter Beardsley. Bobby Robson loved Peter and would always find a place for him in his England team. Robson felt that Lineker and Beardsley were his ideal attacking partnership ever since Peter broke through into the side in place of Mark Hateley during the 1986 World Cup Finals in Mexico. But Peter had a problem with his shin, and had not played for Liverpool for five weeks. There had to be a big question mark over him for the World Cup. Despite denials, Peter had been suffering from a stress fracture.

It was an injury that Liverpool were not too keen to publicize. He had to be very careful because medical opinion is split over such an injury: some experts advise to play on, others suggest that rest is the best remedy. Peter could have played on but he knew the risks. If he got a knock on the injury, the bone could crack; that was the chance he had to take. Of course, it might not crack and he was ready to play for England. After he had rested, Peter was declared fit to play on as the risks had diminished. Bobby Robson urgently needed to find solutions to a growing number of problems. John Barnes had played against Denmark and again against Uruguay up-front and was more successful in defeat against the South Americans.

It was very disappointing that the outstanding unbeaten run had to come to an end, yet England played well against Uruguay. John Barnes scored a great goal; his switch to a more roving, attacking role had worked to a certain extent and that must have edged Robson towards playing him up front in the opening World Cup match against the Irish, but I still felt that the manager was unsure whom to play up front. There was an obvious alternative in Steve Bull, but I had the suspicion that Robson simply didn't fancy Bull as a player, and had no intention of playing him unless it was in an emergency as a substitute.

Thursday 24 May After two days at home, all the players and their wives reported at the hotel ready for departure day to Cagliari on Friday. The plan was for the wives to spend the first week with the players and then leave Sardinia on the same day as the squad moved on to Tunis for their last warm-up match before returning to Cagliari. But, instead of concentrating on the World Cup preparations, we were confronted by a posse of TV cameras, and chased by a pack of press hounds. The hotel was in a state of siege. It was absolute chaos because the news had broken that Bobby Robson would be out as England manager immediately after the World Cup to take up an appointment at PSV Eindhoven. We were being asked our views about Robson and we didn't know a thing.

I've got to be honest and say it took the shine off our get-together with our wives, and departure to the World Cup. However, I don't believe it affected players' performances in the World Cup, but then again neither should it have done. The motivation of playing in the World Cup was all that was needed. If a player lacked that desire, there was no point in him going in the first place. Even the disruption caused by the manner of Robson's departure would not have deflected any of the players from their determination to do well for the country and for themselves.

The confusion over Robson was bad enough but there was also a newspaper story about Paul Gascoigne being involved in a late-night punch-up. It seemed there was trouble wherever you looked. The England manager accepted Gazza's explanation of events outside a Newcastle bar and it did not go any further. Chris Waddle, myself and a few other players were around as Gazza told us what had happened. He is that sort of character; he was anxious to get it off his chest and tell us that he was innocent despite what had been suggested in the papers. He said that a couple of years ago this bloke had tried to have a go at him. When he went back to Newcastle to see his family before leaving for the World Cup, this guy caught up with him outside a night-club as Gazza was getting into his car to drive away. The guy had a go at Gazza. He said to him 'Do you remember me from a couple of years ago?' He was out to cause trouble and start a brawl but Gazza was too quick for him in the punch-up and the aggressor came off worse, but he went crying to the police. Gazza went voluntarily to the police station to explain what had happened.

Friday 25 May   Sir Stanley Matthews waved the team off to Sardinia from Luton Airport as we set off in a plane appropriately named the 'Sir Stanley Matthews'. It was quite an occasion. We were all dressed up in our new England grey suits with our wives or girlfriends on our arms. It should have been such a big day for all of us, but it was all overshadowed by Bobby Robson's own peculiar departure — and still we were in the dark apart from what we all could read about it in the Press. The media focused on the England manager, and it spoilt it for everybody else.

I was impressed by the intensity of the security when we first stepped on to Sardinian soil. I counted three coach-loads of police waiting for us at Cagliari Airport. We had a massive armed guard and a variety of police and security officers escorting our luxury Italia '90 team bus to our hotel nearly an hour's ride outside Cagliari.

As soon as we arrived at our hotel, the England manager called the players to a meeting and he explained that he was sad and upset that the news of his departure had broken before he had the opportunity to tell us first. He said it had been his intention to inform the players and then release the news, but unfortunately for him it had leaked out to the Press.

He told us the reason for his decision to go. It was because the FA refused to guarantee him even another year as England manager once the World Cup had finished and he wasn't going to wait that long. Robson had had an offer from PSV Eindhoven some time earlier and he approached the FA for permission to talk to the Dutch club. That permission was granted to him and the deal was set up.

It all sounded very reasonable and acceptable from Robson's point of view, and no one could blame him for taking the course of action that he did. However, the timing of Robson's decision to go leaves a lot to be desired. It seems pretty naive for someone to believe such news could be kept under wraps until he decided the time was right to release it. There is no doubt in my mind that the Robson business was an unnecessary distraction. It could have been avoided. It was not for me nor any of the players to apportion blame; the matter was between Robson and the FA and it was up to them to sort it out and avoid the sort of unpleasant and ridiculous mix-up we all had to suffer. But the media reaction was incredible, and in some cases well over the top. One paper had a front-page headline accusing Robson of being a 'liar, cheat, and traitor', that he should have been sent to the Tower. They lashed into him and said he wasn't fit to lead England across the road let alone to the World Cup Finals. While that was the sort of garbage Robson often referred to, none the less because of the way his departure was handled, or mishandled, the whole thing was a fiasco, a shambles.

I certainly don't blame Robson for taking refuge abroad. His personal life had come under the microscope in the Press and that must have affected him. But I cannot say whether he took the job on the Continent to escape the persistent hounding from the media about his personal life. Robson held a Press Conference at the FA the day before England left for Cagliari and he was furious at accusations that aspects of his private life had affected his decision to go. He was adamant that that had nothing to do with it.

Robson actually went off to Italy in a 'no-lose' situation. No matter whether England did well or did badly, he was set up with a reputed two-year contract worth £500,000. The players thought that perhaps he would treat the World Cup with a lighter heart, and that he might become a little more lenient, have a laugh and a joke and not care too much about what happened. In fact, if anything, he went to the other extreme. He became even more intense, even more withdrawn, even more anxious to do well. It was as if he was determined to go out as a winner, to prove all his critics wrong, to put two fingers up to those who said he couldn't manage the national team, that he was inflexible and tactically second-division material.

Saturday 26 May The opening week was relaxing, almost a holiday for the players and their wives, at the luxurious Is Morus hotel on the coast. Even so, we trained every day, while the wives went down to the beach for a spot of sunbathing. We trained for an hour and a half to two hours, nothing too strenuous, yet it was still very tiring in the punishing heat. The training I experienced in West Germany prior to the European Championship was excessive, far too hard, and I feel that Robson and his back-room staff learned from that grave mistake. I also understand that the training in Mexico for the last World Cup was similarly too much in the searing heat. I felt that we did an awful lot of work on the training ground in between matches in the European Championships, and that must have contributed to some of the players' fatigue and poor form at the end of a long hard season. The majority of players didn't need such exhausting training as they were fit enough, or at least they should have been. The training in Cagliari was phased down and that might have been one of the reasons for the improvement in performance in the matches.

The routine for the first week was to train in the morning while the wives relaxed, then join them for lunch, and a swim and sunbathe in the afternoon, and then meet up again for an evening meal. Quite frankly, at first I thought it was unwise to take out the wives, but as it turned out I was wrong and it worked exceptionally well. Julie thoroughly enjoyed it, in fact she loved it. I thought it would be a first-rate idea for a group of players within a club environment where all the players and their wives know each other. At international level, the wives would not know the other wives and would be naturally shy and reserved. I thought the whole scheme was fraught with problems and might even lead to trouble between the players, creating cracks in the excellent team spirit, and the players leaving the wives on their own to train would only intensify the problems. However, the wives got along famously and Julie, for example, has made several new friends among the players' wives.

There were only four players who were not accompanied by wives or girlfriends: Trevor Steven, Paul Gascoigne, Chris Waddle and Steve Hodge. Trevor's wife had only just given birth and the baby was too young to be left behind; Gazza's girlfriend didn't accompany him because he wanted to concentrate on the World Cup without any distractions or any excuses for the Press to focus on him even more intensely than they were already; Chris was delayed in France for their Cup semi-finals and Hodgie didn't have a girlfriend at the time. Steve Hodge and Gazza liked to play a lot of tennis or watch videos. The FA brought out plenty of videos and they enjoyed a wide variety, ranging from comedy to horrors, but their favourite was RoboCop.

Players are normally very particular about their food and only want the traditional sort of athletes' fare, such as steak and chips, but the food was excellent, particularly the pasta, and there were no complaints. That was unusual. But, of course, we did bring our own supplies, mostly cereal, sauce and bars of chocolate. Dr John Crane, the England doctor, likes to prescribe a bar of chocolate the night before each match. The majority of players like sauce on their chips, but for once they got stuck into the Italian food. The FA even brought out a £500 water purifier for the hotel to wash the salads. The hotel liked it so much that they bought it from the FA!

Monday 28 May Mark Wright was finally passed fit after several days of anxiety and just 24 hours before the FIFA deadline. Bobby Robson was cautious about his final inclusion until he could see if there was any reaction, but privately he knew Mark had made it. In his daily press conference, the England manager, famous for some of his sayings, commented that Mark was 'seven days better than he was a week ago – and that's not Irish'.

Tuesday 29 May Partly as a publicity exercise and basically designed to keep the England squad match-fit, a friendly was arranged against local side Cagliari on England's training pitch in Pula. Cagliari had been newly promoted to the First Division and the FA had placed adverts in the Sardinia newspapers congratulating them on their achievements. The advert read: 'We wish Sardinia can be as proud of England in the World Cup as they are proud of Cagliari in the Italian League.' Robson had inadvertently angered the locals in Monterrey four years ago when he said that England did not want to play in that particular World Cup centre because of the excessive heat, and that had turned public support against him and his team. This time the FA were determined to get the locals on their side.

As it turned out, the local organizers were unable to sell

tickets because the training stadium had not been completed and they were concerned that it would be a danger to allow the public in. Even so, there must have been 300 people there, with a couple of dozen peering over the fences and 150 police on duty.

For the England manager, this was an opportunity to give the fringe players a run out, although he had to select some first-choice players to make up the numbers. He picked this team: Woods, Stevens, Walker, Parker, Dorigo, Steven, Webb, McMahon, Platt, Beardsley, Bull.

It was an important match for Peter Beardsley in his recovery programme from a stress fracture, but he was clearly lacking in match-fitness. We won 6–0, Steve Bull scored a couple, and I felt I played particularly well. I thought I had done well from the start, and when it got a little physical just before half-time I was able to cope with it.

During the half-time interval, Bobby Robson said to me that we were playing good stuff as a team and he was more than happy with my contribution, but he told me to be a bit careful, be steady, because you never know how these referees will react. He told me to keep it going, that he liked what I was doing.

He told all the players that whatever had been said in the confines of the dressing-room would be 'between us'. He was clearly intimating that we should be discreet and not divulge anything to the Press. You can imagine how shocked I was that the conversation that had taken place between the England manager and myself was back-page news the next day! So much for his insistence on confidentiality. It seemed that he meant that the players couldn't say anything but he was free to say whatever he liked. That was just a little too one-sided for my liking, but I did exactly what everyone else did and obeyed the manager's instructions.

Whether it was exaggerated by the Press, I don't know, but it appears as though Robson had warned me to calm down or risk being sent off, accusing me of being over physical. I did not take it up with the manager, but it did annoy me. I felt I had played reasonably well, and coped with the sort of provocation I was sure we would experience in the World Cup where there would be wide use of intimidation and you would have to know just how far you could go in making the opposition aware that you would not be scared off by it.

Neil Webb, David Platt and I comprised the midfield with anyone having the licence to move forward in a free role, the sort of midfield formation I felt would be ideal for the World Cup action. Because of the selection in this match, it was a foregone conclusion who would be in Robson's starting line-up for the opening match against the Republic. It didn't really matter how well I had played, because I knew that he would start with Paul Gascoigne and Bryan Robson in the centre of the midfield. I accepted that without complaint. It is part of the job. The manager has his opinions and makes his decisions accordingly and it would not have been right to have questioned them either publicly or privately, at least, not at this time.

Thursday 31 May Considering the amount of security personnel surrounding our hotel – it was like a fortress – it was amazing that a photographer had managed to breach the blockade to find his way down to the beach to take long-distance shots of the players and their wives. No one was supposed to be allowed anywhere near our complex without the appropriate permission. The wife of our goalkeeping coach, Mike Kelly, spotted the cameraman hiding between rocks on the beach. Once the alarm was given he sprinted off, chased by five or six security men. He was eventually discovered hiding under a rock with his zoom lens. He was ordered to hand over his film and, as I understand it, he refused but eventually surrendered a roll of film. However, it was a neat trick as it was not the one we wanted.

It wasn't long before we discovered that this Oriental-looking photographer was working for newspapers in England. A prominent picture spread appeared in the *Sunday Mirror*. There was a clever picture of Bobby Robson supposedly eyeing up Chris Woods's wife, and looking as though he was leering at players' wives, portraying him as some sort of pervert. That did not go down too well with our manager considering all the bad publicity he had to endure about his private life. Neither was our skipper very happy, as one can imagine.

This was the first of a couple of serious breaches of privacy, in our view, that created a 'war' between the England party and the media, an unnecessary conflict. From the players' viewpoint, it seemed as if there were journalists and photographers quite prepared to ruin morale in the camp. We simply failed to understand why these people wanted to sabotage our World Cup campaign apart from the obvious excuse that they were doing their job and earning their living, but in the pressure-cooker of a World Cup we were seeking support from the English Press. Instead, we seemed to get the reverse. There was suspicion that they were 'after' Bobby Robson to follow up revelations about his private life. We were unable to relax from this moment on, as after this incident we knew that the media were preying on us and prying into our every move.

Fortunately, our wives were with us and could see for themselves what had happened. The worst part is having to ring them up thousands of miles away to offer explanations. That is when we are most vulnerable.

Friday 1 June The wives fly home on the same day as we fly to Tunis. From this point we got down to the serious business of preparing for the World Cup. The international against Tunisia was the final full-scale warm-up match before the opening World Cup tie with the Irish.

It had always been Robson's intention to play his first-choice team against Tunisia, and he selected: Shilton, Stevens, Butcher, Walker, Pearce, Waddle, Robson, Gascoigne, Hodge, Lineker, Barnes.

But the match did not go according to plan. England's performance was dismal. Terry Butcher head-butted an opponent and was later savagely criticized by Bob Wilson on TV. I cannot condone what Terry had done; no one could. But there were mitigating circumstances that seemed to get overlooked in the hysteria that followed this incident. It was blown out of all proportion. Lots of things happen in the heat of the moment during a match, particularly one of such importance, with the World Cup almost upon us and Terry under immense pressure for his place. But the Tunisian player had been pushing and shoving Terry, dragging him all over the place. All right, that was no excuse for Terry to take matters into his own hands by butting him off the ball just before a free kick. That was blatantly wrong, and Terry deservedly got punished with a booking. He might have even been sent off, but he did not deserve the treatment he got on TV. Unfortunately for the game, television has set itself up as judge and jury. Bob Wilson, an ex-professional, should know better. TV did not focus on any of the provocation, merely the retaliation.

The Tunisian had certainly done his work well because he was not spotted by the referee and he went unpunished. Terry is a tough lad and he can take all the criticism, although it hurt him. However, I felt he was definitely at fault for ripping off his shirt and then throwing it down in disgust when he was brought off later in the game. Every international footballer should wear his shirt with honour and pride. Terry had done just that for many years, shedding blood in England's cause; there were few more patriotic or hyped up when it came to playing for the nation. But it was a terrible gesture to throw down his shirt and I know Terry regretted it immediately he did it.

This was a game to forget all round. We trailed to an early goal after the ball bobbled away from Gazza in midfield and Abdel Hamid Hergal hit a 'wonder' shot from long range that he will never be able to repeat. Just two minutes from the end, substitute Steve Bull came to our rescue with a headed equalizer. Peter Beardsley came on for the final half-hour as a substitute for Steve Hodge and clearly Robson revised his thinking, with England's World Cup only nine days away.

It was particularly frustrating sitting on the bench and not coming on because of the way the team played, but the manager opted to put on Mark Wright for Butcher, David Platt for Waddle, and Beardsley and Bull.

Robson, however, was not unduly concerned when he analysed the match together with the squad. He was more worried that we should get it right against the Irish. But it was here in Tunisia that he decided to scrap his plans to play John Barnes in central attack, reverting to the one-time undisputed first-choice attacking partnership of Lineker and Beardsley, with Barnes back wide on the left.

Immediately after the match, we returned from Tunis to Cagliari, switching to the Is Molas Golf Hotel now that the wives had gone home. We were to be based there for the next three weeks.

Tuesday 5 June We embarked on an hour's journey to Oristano on the Sardinian island to play a Sardinian Select side where the FA launched their message to the fans to behave, with a unique 'own goal' stunt. To promote peace, one of our players would score an own goal from the kick-off to highlight to our supporters that it would be an own goal for English football to cause any trouble during the World Cup in Italy. It had to be a midfield player because the centre-forward would kick off and the next forward would pass it back to midfield. Neil Webb was the first to be asked to perform the 'own goal' honours but he declined – I don't know exactly why. I was asked and I said: 'Why not?' My only concern was that I might miss! It wouldn't be the first time I've gone round the keeper only to put the ball wide!

Before the match we handed out giant sweets to the kids in the crowd and so, too, did Bobby Robson as part of our campaign to win over the Sardinians. Steve Bull kicked off, passed to Peter Beardsley and, in turn, he gave me the ball. I turned, ran on, rounded David Seaman and raised my arm as if it were a proper goal. I don't think that one counted, but the one I got at the end of the match certainly did. We went on to win 10–1, and I scored the tenth. That was the first time I had got on the score sheet for England and it was a special goal for me, particularly as it was also from about thirty yards.

The team was: Seaman, Stevens, Wright, Butcher, Dorigo, Steven, Webb, Platt, McMahon, Beardsley, Bull.

It was a highly satisfying performance from a personal point of view. In fact, I don't think I could have done any more to try to convince the manager that I should be in the World Cup team from the off. Not only did I score, but I seemed to be involved in a number of the goals. But the manager didn't say anything to me, and it was clear that he had already made up his mind about team selection and that this match didn't seem to matter too much, except that it had great significance for just one player, my Liverpool team-mate Peter Beardsley. He confirmed that he was regaining his match-fitness. He didn't score in the first half and that worried Robson, but he came good in the second half with a hat-trick in 17 minutes. That underlined Peter's chances of getting into the starting line-up. Bobby Robson always felt that

Peter was the ideal partner for Gary Lineker and all he needed to do was prove his fitness. Peter mucks in and loves playing for his country. He shares the same background as Bobby Robson, coming from the north-east. But the manager picks him because of his football ability, although it has led to suspicions that Robson had his favourites and showed them tremendous loyalty. Robson likes what Peter does on the field, but he also took a shine to him as a person. That can often happen in football.

Wednesday 6 June   My great claim to fame in this World Cup is winning the players' golf championships sponsored by Wilson. Over nine holes, the players with the six best scores went into a play-off. Seven players scraped through on points: Tony Dorigo, Gary Stevens, Gary Lineker, David Seaman, Paul Gascoigne, David Platt and myself. The venue for the big play-off was the tricky par three hole surrounded by a lake. I felt the best chance of winning was to get on to the green. I got down in three and, with my handicap, it meant a score of two. Tony Dorigo and David Seaman, the two best golfers, didn't have a shot – I had won it. There was one enormous, weighty drawback: for my sins, I had to carry around that heavy marble-based trophy for the next four weeks.

Yet, I was delighted to have won, but there was more pressure out there on the golf-course than in any big match I've played in! In fact, I would rather have played in front of 40,000 at Anfield any time. All the players, the manager and the TV crews were there and it was played in a tremendously competitive spirit. But it was also great fun and a superb way to relax.

We also had a putting competition – and I won that. But I failed to get the treble, because John Barnes, a non-golfer, won the longest drive competition. All credit to Wilson: they sent out a professional for a few days to provide some lessons and they also supplied us with a set of clubs. John didn't enter the first two competitions and, instead, took a concentrated half an hour's coaching from the pro on the driving range. It certainly worked. He cracked a 315-yard drive. Even some of the top golf professionals in the world manage no more than 280- to 290-yard drives in the big tournaments.

It was very embarrassing — we got so much stick with Liverpool sweeping the board of all the silverware again!

Chapter 14

World Cup Diary: Bryan Robson's Exit

IT SEEMS ALMOST INEVITABLE that the start of England's World Cup campaign should be shrouded in the uncertainty of yet another Bryan Robson injury drama.

Thursday 7 June The team trained normally but with anticipation growing with the big game now only days away. It was long after our training session and supposedly back at the safety of our team hotel that Bryan injured himself! He stubbed his toe in the bathroom, slipping onto the bidet. The toe-nail came right off and the skin along with it. It was a nasty, very painful injury and Bryan was struggling to be fit for our opening World Cup tie against the Republic of Ireland on Monday.

Bobby Robson had experienced such agonies with Bryan four years ago in Mexico, where he covered up the extent of the England skipper's shoulder injury prior to the tournament, and it was no different this time as he was eager to mask the extent of Bryan's latest injury problem. The England manager disguised the full extent of Bryan's injury very well, and it seemed incredible that Bryan's absence in training was not missed too much by anybody. We all knew that it was really bad but we were also aware that it had to be kept under wraps.

day 8 June Italia '90 kicked off with the opening match between the World Champions, Argentina, and the true dark horses of the tournament, Cameroon. Courtesy of the BBC, we were provided with a giant screen in our team hotel with English commentary to watch all the World Cup matches we wanted to, and we all enjoyed jeering at the commentators' mistakes. None of us who sat down to watch what turned out to be such a spectacular opening game could possibly have imagined that we would be cheering our heads off in appreciation of the Cameroons' remarkable performance against Diego Maradona and his World Champions.

When Omam Biyak scored for the Cameroons we were all leaping up and down in the air and screaming with delight. It was an incredible goal − I couldn't believe how high he leapt to head the ball, it was an amazing feat. To be perfectly honest, everyone in that room, every single player was more pleased that Argentina lost than the Cameroons won. We would all have been delighted had the Argentinians lost, no matter who they had been playing. (Certainly, no one dreamed that very shortly we would be playing Cameroon or, indeed, have an outstanding chance of playing Argentina in the World Cup Final.)

It was all the more remarkable that the Cameroons had pulled off one of the biggest surprises of all time in the World Cup Finals as they had Kana Biyak sent off, brother of the goal scorer.

Sunday 10 June Bobby Robson selected his team for the opening match, much as we all expected, with Peter Beardsley reinstated in the side alongside Gary Lineker, John Barnes in the wide position, with Chris Waddle on the opposite flank. But there was one major surprise, as the England manager named his team with skipper Bryan Robson or me in midfield. The manager told me that I could be playing and that there was every chance that I would be, that he was unsure about Bryan's ability to get over his toe injury, the full extent of which he had still to tell anybody.

Monday 11 June   ENGLAND v. REPUBLIC OF IRE-LAND

Bryan Robson had an injection before the game and tested out his toe and, although it was still very painful, he decided to play. I was on the bench. The manager was back to his old team and, although he switched to the sweeper system for the very next match and stuck with it for the rest of the tournament, in my view this was the ideal game to play a sweeper system, if indeed that's what he was going to do. I would have played Mark Wright from the start, particularly when the Irish had players like Tony Cascarino and John Aldridge up-front. It would have then meant sacrificing one of the wide men, either John Barnes or Chris Waddle, or even relying on Gary Lineker alone up-front and leaving out Peter Beardsley.

Yes, it was an awful game, of that there could be no dispute, but I always expected the game to be like that, a match between two teams of British style and attitudes. I was shocked that few people saw it that way from the start and complained about the way the match was conducted, the style of play in the context of the World Cup. I don't know why anyone should have complained. We all knew what it was going to be like and I agreed when the manager commented, 'Let's see if the other teams in this World Cup competition can perform any better against the Irish, considering the sort of problems they will pose.'

However, there was a very pleasant and pleasing aspect of the entire occasion. We arrived at the ground a couple of hours before the kick-off to find the Irish fans had filled their end of the stadium. They were singing and dancing, thoroughly enjoying themselves and gave everybody a great welcome, including us.

They were certainly supporting their team in the true sense of the word and it was a joy to behold.

Gary Lineker gave us the perfect start to our World Cup campaign with a goal after just 18 minutes, his 32nd goal for his country and his seventh in World Cup competition.

After 69 minutes, Bobby Robson decided to make a substitution, bringing me on in place of Peter Beardsley. The England manager made a tactical substitution because Jack Charlton had moments earlier brought on Swindon's midfield player McLoughlin, and Bobby Robson was concerned that the Irish would cause us problems in midfield. My job was to tighten up that area of the field and to ensure that the Irish didn't score and that we began the World Cup with two points. It had been a frustrating time watching from the bench, particularly as the game was not inspiring, but I had only been on the field for four minutes when the ball came to me just outside our penalty area and it ran away from me straight to my Merseyside foe, Kevin Sheedy from Everton, who gleefully took his opportunity by rifling the ball into the corner of the net.

Devastated. Sheer devastation. It was one of the worst moments, perhaps the worst, in my entire footballing career. I was so desperate to play for my country in the World Cup and there I was, only a few minutes on the pitch, when I had given away a vital goal.

I was determined to get on with it, to get it out of my system, to play well enough to put it all right. But clearly I did not pull myself together. Just two minutes later I got myself booked, the first yellow card for England in the World Cup. It was all very silly: a scuffle with Paul McGrath in midfield, one of the sort of incidents that occur so regularly in the First Division and with that same player, and 99 times out of 100 nothing would happen. But in this World Cup we had already seen from the outset some incredible refereeing decisions and this was another one of them.

It had just gone from bad to worse for me. I had let down the team and got myself booked. The manager didn't say very much to me immediately after the game; he didn't need to. In the dressing-room I held my hands up and I apologized to him and to the rest of the team; I owned up that it was my mistake for the goal.

I read the manager's comments in the Press: 'Steve McMahon made a mistake, he got punished for it and that's it. The boy didn't do it on purpose. It was a team error. He just miscontrolled the ball and the wrong player (Sheedy) got it. He's good at hitting them low. I feel sorry for McMahon. He was so pleased to get on and it was tactically right to protect our 1–0 lead; the Italians do it, the Germans do it. The ball was very wet and difficult to control and it was a vital touch not long after coming on.'

When Robson was asked what he planned to say to me he responded: 'I haven't got to him yet.'

I can't blame Robson for being disappointed in me, I was so disappointed in myself.

Tuesday 12 June   I knew in my own heart that I would not get another chance in the next match against Holland and probably never again in this World Cup competition. I could hardly sleep, I was that sick with myself and for my family.

The Republic of Ireland game was my 13th cap for England and, yes, you could say it was unlucky. My World Cup had started in the worst possible way. It was not an easy task to try to lift myself up, but I knew that's what I had to do. I had to be professional, I had to believe in myself, I had to convince myself that I would get another chance here in Italy and I would prove to the rest of the world, to the people back home, to my team-mates and to the manager that I could play a useful part for England in this World Cup competition. Fortunately, I'm not the type of person that wilts easily and here was a time I had to dig deep into myself to find new sources of resolve. It was not easy, and I also knew how much my family and friends were suffering along with me.

Funnily enough, a TV interview with the new England manager elect, Graham Taylor, helped to lift my depression. Naturally, I was the person that everyone in the media wanted to speak to the next day and, equally naturally, I was reluctant to talk, but I did agree to give one interview and one interview only on TV. I explained how awful I felt because I wanted everyone to know that, and I said on TV: 'I was very excited and dying to get on, but when I did, I wished I'd stayed on the bench. The dressing-room was a very depressing place. It was a body blow. I feel as guilty as anybody would do in the circumstances. We were winning 1–0 and I knew I was thrown on to help hold the lead. It was very disappointing that the incident involved me. It's very difficult to control the way the Irish play but we found it difficult to get out of our own box, never mind playing football.'

Graham Taylor was then introduced as part of the programme and, I suppose to break the ice, I said: 'Should I call you Graham or should I call you boss, especially after last night!' Graham Taylor replied: 'It's good to see your smiling face. That's what worried me, that you might be depressed, but at Liverpool they bounce back and I'm sure England will as well.'

Graham Taylor was in the studios in London but he was keen to tell me to keep my head up and when he said he didn't want to talk about football to me, that all he was interested in was that I shouldn't be worried, that helped me. His attitude was 'these things happen'. Bobby Robson's message to me was much the same, if a little briefer! I suppose it must have been much harder for the England manager, with so many other things going through his mind, to talk to me immediately after the game but he did approach me this day. He said: 'Never mind, that's the way it is.'

All that helped me, but there was still a deep feeling of depression because I was a million miles away from home and so much races through your mind. All I really wanted, all I was praying for, was for another opportunity to repay everybody for my mistake. But it crossed my mind, more than once, that the England manager may have lost faith in me.

Wednesday 13 June   The most upsetting newspaper story of them all broke and it really affected the players badly. It was suggested that three or four of the England players had disgraced themselves in a hotel bedroom with Italia '90 hostess Isabella Ciaravolo. We had heard that the *Sun* newspaper had offered the girl £20,000 for her side of the story; the reality was that they were making her an offer to lie. She turned down that approach but the story still appeared on the front pages of two or three papers, including a front-page lead article in the *Mirror*. As far as I knew, the girl could speak hardly a word of English and that's why she had been transferred from the England team hotel to another post at another hotel.

This sort of story only strengthened the players' belief that there was an orchestrated campaign in some quarters to undermine our World Cup effort. Whether or not that was true is hard to assess but, with the stress and strain and concentration of the World Cup, that's how it felt to us. This story was a total fabrication and it was diabolical that English newspapers should carry it at the outset of our World Cup.

I rang my wife Julie immediately the story appeared, even though I knew she wouldn't believe a word of it. The papers had said that four players had been involved in high jinx, but didn't name those players and that meant it could have been any one of us. It is never easy explaining it's not you to your wife who's thousands of miles away. Those articles pointed the finger at every player in the England camp. Although they didn't actually say what the papers wanted to say, by innuendo they left little to the imagination.

It almost got worse as the Italian papers were alerted to the story, and one or two actually named names. The players who were in the firing line were John Barnes, Chris Waddle, Paul Gascoigne and Stuart Pearce, and I believe one or two were ready to take legal action.

I don't for one minute believe even something as crude and unwarranted as this would have any effect on the players' ability to perform to their optimum on the pitch, but you never know, it could have done. It became laughable, in fact, when the girl threatened to go to a doctor to prove she was still a virgin! I think that shut a few people up.

The impact that morning on the players was immense, so much so that they wanted nothing more to do with the Press. The England manager was quoted as saying: 'The players wouldn't want to share the same ground as people who have written such garbage, that's why they've gone.'

We all elected to get on to the coach immediately after training and were whisked off to our hotel. By the time the Press arrived, the training ground was deserted; we had gone. The manager said that we should speak to the Press. Bobby Robson was the most vilified manager of all time in English soccer history but, despite all the blows, he was prepared to come back for more and carry on his relationship with the media. But Peter Shilton and Bryan Robson and one or two of the other more experienced players said that it should be left up to the individuals. There were problems, of course, because some players had contracts with newspapers which had to be honoured, but it was up to the others whether or not they spoke to the Press. It was almost unanimous that they didn't want anything to do with them, so we all got on the bus and went off. That set a trend for the rest of the trip. We were all too eager to get on the bus as quickly as possible and have as little to do with the media as we could. I don't know how you can blame the players for that after the way that we had been treated.

Thursday 14 June   During the days preceding a World Cup match we would watch videos of the opposition, and we studied the style and methods of the Dutch team. However, I don't think this did much good, considering that Holland had almost totally altered the structure of their team as so many players had lost confidence since they beat England in the European Championships in West Germany two years earlier, and there had been much wrangling behind the scenes and managerial changes.

Friday 15 June   Bobby Robson was deeply worried about the pace of Marco Van Basten and Ruud Gullit and, for that reason, just 24 hours before facing Holland, the England manager decided to experiment with a sweeper system. That's how much notice the players got of his new system. Not that Robson was even sure that he was going to use it, after trying it out just a day before the game.

When he announced the team later that evening it was a surprise, even a shock. He decided to leave out Peter Beardsley and Gary Stevens and he brought in Paul Parker as an attacking right-back and Mark Wright as the sweeper.

I don't believe for one minute that you can just go into a World Cup tie of this magnitude playing an entirely new system, particularly in such a vital area of the field, virtually off the cuff. It would have made far more sense to have used one or two of the far less meaningful warm-up games to have experimented with the system. Why not have tried it out against Denmark or

Uruguay at Wembley where it would have been ideal preparation if the manager thought that he might use it in the World Cup at any stage? It is my firm conviction that Bobby Robson never dreamed of using the sweeper system in the World Cup Finals and always intended to stick by his tried and trusted four at the back. I have a feeling that it was all forced upon him, with so many people suggesting that it should be used — the media and the players. I feel that the manager succumbed to the pressure, but was neither sure about using it nor convinced that it would work. The whole thing was sheer nonsense. You can argue that the players who were asked to perform the sweeper system had experience of it at club level at various times in their careers, but surely at such short notice to develop an understanding in the England structure was a necessity and, of course, it should have been tried in a full-scale match, not just on the training field.

I suppose the England manager could argue that he wanted to keep the sweeper system under wraps. Well, he succeeded so thoroughly that not even the players knew anything about it! I'm convinced that he always intended to use the system he knew best, 4–4–2, throughout the World Cup. Robson had been accused of being inflexible and perhaps he wanted to show everyone who had been criticizing him for years that he had some tactical awareness. Fortunately, there was so much pace at the back, with players like Mark Wright, Des Walker and Paul Parker, that it was able to work. Personally, I would have retained Gary Stevens at right-back to utilize his pace on the flank. The manager could have left Terry Butcher out of the team but chose not to, sticking loyally to his big centre-half.

Although it was suggested that few clubs play the sweeper system back home, that is a fallacy as well. Liverpool have utilized it, and quite successfully at times, and so, too, have leading clubs like Arsenal, Spurs and Aston Villa. But the problem is that not all the players came from one club. We had the right players, we had the pace, the only question mark was whether it would all gel together.

Saturday 16 June ENGLAND v. HOLLAND

As it turned out, the new-look team played superbly well. We produced an outstandingly professional performance against the Dutch and, although it was goalless, it put us *en route* for qualification. There can be no doubt that the new system convinced the England manager that it was the right one for the World Cup. However, it did not go according to the manager's plans. The Dutch surprised Robson with their attacking formation and the predominantly left-footed Butcher ended up playing right-back for the first time in his career, as it was the intention to play Parker in an advanced position down the right where the manager considered Trevor Steven. Yet, Butcher adapted remarkably well in this unorthodox role for him and even made some vital headed interceptions and clearances when he was called upon to move back into the middle of defence.

This was the match in which Peter Shilton became the new world-record holder of international caps with 120, and it was also the game which served only to increase my depression over my mistake against the Irish. Skipper Bryan Robson was substituted, but it was David Platt who was the man chosen to come on rather than me, with young Paul Gascoigne outstanding in midfield. I was more inclined to think from that moment on that that was the end of my World Cup.

It had always been the accepted principle that if Bryan Robson was out injured or unavailable, I would be his replacement in midfield. All of a sudden, that role had been handed over to David Platt. It was particularly hard to accept as I was so desperately keen to get over my disappointment for my mistake against the Irish. As I sat on the bench, it didn't make sense to me at the time, but I had to accept that it didn't work out too badly. I felt it would have been justified to have put me on as substitute to allow Gazza to continue to make life difficult for the Dutch. The England manager explained his decision to the media after the game, revealing that he put on Platt to 'track the big fellow' (Gullit). Robson went on: 'Platt was the best man on the substitutes' bench to let Gazza have his head and run the show. I said not "Macca", but Platt can do the job on Gullit.'

While it was one hell of a week for me, it was certainly just as agonizing for Bryan Robson. He needed pain-killing injections to overcome his toe injury and now he had gone off with an Achilles problem. The England manager admitted that he didn't know how bad it was, but as the days went by it became more obvious that the skipper was not going to make it. I made a note in my diary immediately after the Holland match that 'I'm paying for my mistake against the Irish and only time will tell if I'll ever get the chance to make amends'.

Sunday 17 June We had four days' break before our final group match against Egypt and during this time we had a series of 'race nights'. We used those old-fashioned films that are so popular at holiday camps such as Butlins. No one knew the results and you'd have a bet on the number of the horse. Gary Lineker and Peter Shilton were always the bookies, making the odds and taking all the bets. They even did this on all the World Cup matches, taking odds on the results and placing bets on the goal scorers.

Monday 18 June The race nights were always great fun and, on this particular occasion, we decided to get our own back on the bookies who seemed to be making a killing. Our physio, Fred Street, had supplied us with the tapes. We decided to find out the result of one of the races and not to let on to the bookies. Bryan Robson and Paul Gascoigne bet heavily on horse number five while a few others played along by just putting their usual £10 on the other horses.

When horse number five romped in the clear winner, Peter Shilton almost collapsed with shock, he couldn't believe it. He'd lost £1,500. All the lads walked out of the room and we could all see that Peter Shilton and Gary Lineker were devastated. We couldn't keep it to ourselves for much longer, but when we told them they went berserk, they nearly had a heart attack! I wouldn't dare repeat what they called us.

This was just one of the many examples of the tremendous team spirit that had built up within the camp. All these sorts of pranks were taken in good spirit – eventually! We all looked after each other, we all helped each other, and none more so than Gazza who needed special attention. In fact, the England manager told us before the World Cup started that he had warned Gazza to take it easy and he told all of us that if Gazza got any funny ideas, got up to any mischief, it was up to us to restrain him because the manager couldn't be watching him 24 hours a day. That was fair enough but it did put the onus on us a bit.

Tuesday 19 June Bryan Robson was still struggling with his Achilles, and he knew it was quite bad, but at this stage he still didn't know just how bad. He felt that with a few days' rest it might clear up. He knew that there was little point playing against Egypt on the Thursday, but he now became deeply concerned about whether he would be able to continue in the World Cup at all. For that reason, he contacted a faith healer he knew very well, Olga Stringfellow. He believed in her because he had been treated by her in the past and it seemed to work for him. Although it seemed an extreme measure to fly her over from England to our team hotel in Cagliari, Bryan was obviously very distressed and ready to try anything. Because it was the World Cup it was all hyped up. It was clear that Olga was interested in self-publicity and it all turned out to be a publicity stunt on her behalf.

Wednesday 20 June I didn't really want to get back into the England team because of the misfortune of Bryan Robson, but that's the way it turned out and you have to take your chance. I was bursting to get that chance and it was a great relief to be named in the team. It was a vital match for England. We needed to win to ensure our qualification, but also to top the group for the perfect route to the World Cup Semi-Finals, and perhaps the Final itself. Everyone was anxious that we shouldn't allow ourselves to be left wide open to the drawing of lots. Our instructions from the England manager were not to do anything stupid, to avoid believing we could go out and swamp Egypt; our priority was to ensure we didn't lose, knowing that we would be strong from our set pieces, and to cause them problems.

The England manager had hinted strongly that he would play me because he had been saying: 'I need a player who understands Gazza.' My function, as it had been in the build-up to the World Cup before we left for Italy, was to protect Gazza and allow him to go forward.

Thursday 21 June ENGLAND v. EGYPT

England had never lost to a Third World team and we had no intention of making history for the wrong reasons. Unfortunately, we started very slowly and it was a very disappointing opening half-hour for us. It was dour and uninspired. But, from a personal point of view, my confidence grew and my partnership with Gazza began to cement and I was even able to start coming out of my 'hole' a little bit more.

The only surprise in the team selection was that Steve Bull was playing, with Terry Butcher left out. There had been plenty of pressure to drop Butcher but the manager kept faith with him up until this match. However, Terry was struggling with a knee injury and that may have been the reason for his omission. The sweeper system had been a huge success against Holland, but Robson switched back to a flat back four against Egypt, perhaps his argument being that he wanted to go for the victory and that's why Bull got his one and only chance from the start. Once again, although there seemed to be little logic to Bobby Robson's team selections, they turned out to be the right ones.

Des Walker was fouled by Ibrahim Hassan, and Gazza curled a perfect free kick for Mark Wright to soar above the keeper and head into the corner for his first goal for his country. Bobby Robson made the point: 'Holland and Ireland couldn't beat Egypt, we just have. It was a very tight group, the tightest of the lot, with no one capable of scoring many goals. It was a vital header, Walker was outstanding and Gazza produced some great passes. But Egypt were good enough to always have England on a knife-edge.'

As for my performance, the England manager said: 'McMahon did a very steady job and played pretty well and I quite liked what he did once he settled in.' I felt I did OK. I was steady Eddie.

When I got back to the dressing-rooms after swapping shirts with an Egyptian, I looked at the back and it was No. 13. I felt at last I had got my 13th cap against the Irish out of my system.

Chapter 15

World Cup Diary:
The Glory and the Rows

Saturday 23 June It was late on Saturday evening when we first discovered that Bryan Robson was going back home. He didn't really want to tell anybody, and who could blame him? The England manager would have preferred to keep it quiet and let him slip away without any fuss, and Bobby Robson tried his best once again to maintain a high level of secrecy. However, it was virtually impossible to keep something like this quiet for long. At dinner that night Bryan wished everybody all the best and hoped we would go on to win the World Cup. He spoke briefly to us all and it was crystal clear just how disappointed he was. After all the traumas of the World Cup four years ago in Mexico this must have really hurt him deeply.

All the players were choked for Bryan. We didn't realize just how bad his Achilles injury was until he told us that he was going home. At first he thought that he would miss a game or two and then he would be playing again. Now he was going back for an operation, worrying that if it was as bad as Neil Webb's, who had missed the vast majority of the season after an Achilles operation, there would be a serious question mark over whether he would ever play again for his country. As it was, he was going back knowing there would be a change in manager and that he would have to make a rapid recovery from his operation to stand any chance at all of representing England again.

Sunday 24 June The fact that we had finished top of our group meant that we were able to remain in our hotel in Cagliari for an extra few days, but now it was finally time to leave our 'home' base to move on for the knock-out phase of the tournament – but we were moving on without our skipper. Bryan Robson departed well ahead of the rest of the party, leaving at the crack of dawn to avoid as much hassle as possible. Bryan left our team hotel at 7.45 a.m., accompanied by manager Bobby Robson, to catch the 9.15 flight from Cagliari to Milan and then make the onward journey home to Manchester. It must have been a miserable flight for Bryan on the Alisarda DC9 super 80 jet flight taking him on the first leg of the journey to Milan. Wearing a T-shirt and jeans and trying to look as inconspicuous as possible, he couldn't even drown his sorrows – it was a dry plane!

Monday 25 June Although we were pleased to stay on a little longer in Cagliari it was none the less a pleasant change of environment to switch to our Nova hotel in Bologna. We felt at home there, with a large swimming-pool and tennis court and all that we needed. We knew how important the match with Belgium was going to be, with Cameroon waiting at the Quarter-Final stage. Before the tournament started, England, or any of the top nations, would have settled for a confrontation against the Cameroons in the last eight with a great hope of a Semi-Final place and the Final itself beckoning.

Bobby Robson picked his team, reinstating Terry Butcher in defence and making him skipper as well. It had been 54 years since Belgium last beat England and we had no intention of letting them do it again. But not only had our skipper gone home, the tournament so far had taken its toll. Gary Lineker was training in his slippers, still suffering the effects of a sore toe injury. He needed an injection before the Egypt match and he was in a great deal of pain afterwards. It was hard to assess how much of his sharpness and edge had been lost because of this injury. Des Walker had been whacked into an advertising board by an Egyptian tackle and was suffering a swelling of the side of his ankle; John Barnes had a medial knee-ligament strain, and it was a case of patching them up and sending them out.

The England manager emphasized his disappointment at the loss of his skipper when he said: 'I'm very disappointed for the player, naturally. He's always been a great example on the pitch and we're going to miss him, but we've got to get over it and get him out of our minds. He can't help us now and that's unfortunate. I thought he would be absolutely marvellous in this World Cup, in fact I was excited about him and I can't believe it's happened to him again.'

Also, in his Press Conferences leading up to the Belgium match, it seemed clear that Robson was happy with my performance against Egypt when he said: 'McMahon played well the other night after a nervous first 20 minutes. He proved he could handle the situation, got better in the second half and was quite good for Gazza.'

Once again, we suffered unnecessary bad publicity for a minor incident that occurred when the Press were at our training ground. Paul Parker was giving an interview and Gazza threw something at him. The Press seemed to think it was a Coke can, but it turned out to be a Coke cup. They were under the impression that Gazza was trying to break up the interview, when in fact he was larking about as usual. It made front-page news, but there was nothing in it. After what had happened in recent days this was no more than a minor irritation, but once again emphasized the rift between the players and the media. There had also been an article about John Barnes suggesting that his inability to convert his scintillating performances for Liverpool into an England shirt was due to some problem in his past with his mother. That only served to annoy John who is a very sensitive man.

Bobby Robson was at pains to play down the impact of Paul Gascoigne before the Belgium match and called upon others, who had come to the World Cup with far bigger reputations than Gazza, to play their part.

Tuesday 26 June   ENGLAND v. BELGIUM

In part I felt it was a very good England performance. But, in all honesty, the game could have gone either way and at the end Belgium must have felt very disappointed indeed to have gone out of the World Cup. If we had played as well as Belgium and been eliminated, we'd have been sick. It was an evenly fought contest and perhaps just unfortunate that one team had to go out.

My instructions were to ensure that Belgium's danger man, 24-year-old Enzo Scifo, was kept as quiet as possible. As usual, my role was to sit in the hole behind Gazza and to pick up Scifo. Despite his age, he was a very experienced campaigner having already moved from Belgian to Italian football with Inter Milan before switching to Bordeaux and now trying to resurrect his career at Auxerre. Granted Scifo saw a lot of the ball during the match, but I had to get on with my own game, too, and help to protect Gazza; my assignment was not just to follow Scifo around all over the place. I restricted him to just a couple of shots, although one was a spectacular curler that struck our post. Other than that, I felt he was ineffective. I had the option of trying to dispossess him when he was on the ball but if I dived in and missed out I would expose our defence. I tended to shadow him and ensure that he was always in front of me where I could see him, so that I kept him at a distance, curtailing him to 30- or 40-yard shots. I thoroughly enjoyed the experience and for the first time I really felt part of the England team. No disrespect to Bryan Robson, I felt that I had done my bit to ensure that we did not miss him. I knew this was my big chance to stake a claim and I felt I had taken it.

Peter Shilton made a very important save as early as the second minute, from Versavel, and Chris Waddle had a very impressive spell in the opening half. Shilton also made a very important save from Ceulemans after Wright was unlucky with a challenge. It was after Scifo struck the post in the 50th minute that we had our most worrying spell, and in the 72nd minute Bobby Robson decided to take me off and bring on David Platt. John Barnes then pulled up and it wasn't long before he came off and was replaced by Steve Bull. Butcher hurt his knee launching into a tackle and Walker damaged his ankle from a fierce challenge by Belgium substitute Nico Claessen, the one-time Spurs player. Gazza was booked for a tackle on Scifo just three minutes before the end of normal time and Walker could hardly run. It was a minute before the end of extra time, with a penalty shoot-out looming, when Gazza made his spectacular break before being brought down. Gazza got up and chipped a perfect free kick over the defence and into the path of Platt who turned and hooked the ball into the corner for England's winner.

Bobby Robson said it was a difficult decision to take me off and bring on David Platt but the Aston Villa skipper came on and scored. No doubt, that made Robson think about Platt's chances against Cameroon in the World Cup Quarter-Final.

Saturday 30 June Bobby Robson picked his team, and Platt was in and I was out. The England manager said he wanted more going forward in midfield against Cameroon. I accepted it without question at the time but deep down it got my back up. I knew that my style of play was going forward, that's what I do for Liverpool and, without trying to sound big-headed, I do it successfully and have done for several years. But I accepted it.

It was interesting that Bobby Robson told us that he had a full report from his scouts about the capabilities of the first African nation to get so far in the World Cup Finals. He told us that if we played 'half decent and get at them the game is almost a bye'. He based that assessment on a report from one of his scouts who was obviously not very impressed by Cameroon.

Sunday 1 July ENGLAND v. CAMEROON

Well, as it turned out it was almost bye-bye England! Far from being a bye, the Cameroons surprised everyone. I remember as the two teams waited to leave the tunnel before the start of the match, their players were singing loudly and it sounded like some sort of war dance; they were giving it everything and looked keyed up to beat England. Bobby Robson walked out in front of us and said: 'They can't sing, and they can't play.' Roger Milla, their 38-year-old sub who had already scored four goals in the tournament, was one of several of the Cameroon team who could obviously speak perfect English. He replied: 'Who can't play?' And Roger Milla and his team went out and demonstrated that they can play.

Even though the Cameroons had four players banned they proved to be a handful. England got off to a perfect start with my replacement getting the opening goal after just 26 minutes. Terry Butcher played the pass down the flank for Stuart Pearce whose perfect cross was met by Platt to give us the lead that we wanted. Cameroon super-sub Roger Milla, who had been called up for the World Cup on the orders of the Minister of Sport, came on in the second half and made an instant impact, winning a penalty in the 61st minute after a challenge by Gazza. It was a harsh decision, but Gazza showed his inexperience by making the challenge in such a vulnerable position, and although Peter Shilton got both hands to the ball he couldn't stop Kunde's penalty. Five minutes later, Roger Milla split the England defence and Cameroon's other substitute, Eugene Ekek Ebelle, put the Africans ahead. Stuart Pearce was booked and Terry Butcher was taken off in the 74th minute, with Trevor Steven coming on as the England manager drastically reshaped his team.

England were just eight minutes away from going out of the World Cup when Gary Lineker was brought down and he got up to equalize from the penalty spot. Mark Wright got a nasty cut eye as the game went into extra time. Once again it was Gazza who produced an exhilarating run when you would have thought he'd have been on his last legs. It was Gazza's throughball for Lineker that produced our second penalty, and Lineker changed his penalty style: having placed the first one, he smashed this one past their keeper for our winner.

England had ridden their luck, Lineker had lost a stone in weight with the effort, the rest of the team has lost around half a stone each, Walker could hardly walk at the end, and Wright needed six stitches and a protective covering before he could play again. Barnes was out of the tournament – but we had got to the World Cup Semi-Finals. It was the first time in our history that we had reached the World Cup Semi-Finals on foreign soil. It was a time for celebration, but also there was a determination to beat West Germany in the Semi-Finals.

Tuesday 3 July Bobby Robson selected his World Cup Semi-Final team on the training ground where Ian Rush used to prepare for matches in pre-season for Juventus, outside Turin. The England manager gathered all his players round on the pitch and announced his team. I was not in it, and I was not happy. I never said anything when I was dropped for the Cameroon game, I bit my lip then, but I couldn't do that again now. I told Bobby Robson that I needed to have a word with him, and there were still a few players around when I had my say.

I began: 'What's the situation? I accepted that you left me out against Cameroon but when you look at that match they could have been 3–1 up at half-time, the number of chances they created.'

He simply said: 'Yes.' He then explained to me in detail that he had left me out because he wanted a midfield player supporting Paul Gascoigne going forward more. My grievance was that because they had two attacking midfield players, they had left so many gaps for Cameroon to exploit and that was the reason why they created so many chances. The West Germany match was ideal for me to sit in the hole as I had been doing, protecting Gazza and letting him go forward to attack the Germans.

Bobby Robson said: 'We all have our opinions and there are a lot of players who are not in the team who think they should be.'

I put it to him: 'If Bryan Robson had still been here you'd have played Bryan Robson in the holding midfield position.'

Robson agreed: 'That's true, I would have played Bryan there.'

It was my turn: 'Why don't you play me there, if that's the case? I'm supposed to be Bryan Robson's replacement. I can do that job.'

Robson responded: 'David Platt came on for you and has scored goals for me and that's why I'm sticking by him.'

I wasn't giving up: 'Does that mean that if you score a goal you're in the team no matter what else you do?' I wasn't having a go at any individual. I wasn't criticizing his decision to play David Platt. But I just couldn't make out his strategy. This was not a nicey-nicey conversation. We weren't shouting but you could call it a lively discussion. I just felt I was banging my head against a brick wall; I knew he wouldn't change his mind but I had to get it off my chest, I had to say something.

I finally said: 'I know there's nothing I can do about this; you pick the team. But if you're talking about wanting a player to go forward, I can do that as well. It's not my style to sit in the hole, I don't do that at Liverpool, you must have watched me play many times for Liverpool and you know I'm a player that always goes forward.'

In fact, I've averaged between 10 and 12 goals a season in my five years at Liverpool. I had to accept that David Platt had come on and scored for England and that had made Bobby Robson change his mind. But I had always played to the England manager's instructions, I had done what he'd asked of me and now I was looking for something in return. I was not happy with his explanation but what could I do about it?

I just felt that the deficiencies against Cameroon had been glossed over, covered up if you like, by the fact that we actually won the game and that the whole team had done their part. Yet, with just over seven minutes to go we were really dead and buried against Cameroon and we were lucky to get through. However, you need luck in any Cup competition and we weren't complaining about that. I just hoped that the England manager would not have worn blinkers over his eyes and felt that there was no room for improvement against West Germany. Because of the number of chances we conceded against Cameroon I felt we needed to stiffen up our midfield against the Germans. Perhaps this was a selfish attitude on my part and, as the match unfolded the next day, really I could complain no longer.

Wednesday 4 July   ENGLAND v. WEST GERMANY

I was told that there were nearly 30 million people watching on TV back home, that the whole country came to a virtual standstill to watch us. If everyone was so excited back home, you can imagine how excited we felt taking part. We were confronting the most experienced World Cup nation of all time, playing a record 67th game in the finals, surpassing a record set by Brazil. It was the German's ninth Semi-Final, another record; there could be no tougher task than taking on Franz Becken-bauer's team in the Stadio Delle Alpi.

The manager never played the same team, or the same formation, two games running. With Mark Wright needing protection because of his head wound, he switched Butcher to the sweeper role while Wright and Walker were the man-to-man markers on Klinsmann and Voeller.

England got off to a fabulous start. We seemed to be in control in the early exchanges. Talk about our luck, the Germans got the break in the 59th minute when Olaf Thon's short free kick was struck by Andreas Brehme and wickedly deflected off Paul Parker's foot. Peter Shilton got a hand to it, but as he fell backwards he couldn't stop it going in. You could see the relief on the faces of the manager and the players on the German bench. With 10 minutes remaining, Lineker came to our rescue again with his 10th goal in two World Cup campaigns, his fourth in this tournament and his 35th for his country to take us into extra time.

When Gazza was needlessly booked by Brazilian referee José Ramiz Wright in the eighth minute of extra time, and he knew he would have been out of the Final, he was emotionally and physically shattered. He knew it was the end of his competition, and I would have brought him off there and then. You could see that he'd had enough. The booking decision was clawing on his mind. His legs were going. For the sake of the team it would have been better to put on a fresh pair of legs. In fact, I warmed up a couple of times after Gazza was booked but the England manager decided to leave him on. Good luck to him. I thought Gazza had an exceptional World Cup, better than he expected, better than anyone really expected. I was delighted for him, but I felt that the manager should have looked ahead to the next game, whether that be the Final of the World Cup or the play-off for third and fourth place, and brought him off. On reflection, I would have played in the World Cup Final if England had got there, taking the place of Paul Gascoigne.

We had our moments to win in extra time when Chris Waddle shot against the inside of the post but, with three minutes to go, Buchwald curled a shot against the post as well. Gazza collapsed in a flood of tears at the final whistle and the whole nation felt sorry for him. Bobby Robson tried to console him as the penalty shoot-out began.

Gary Lineker set the tone by sending the keeper the wrong way and that was a good start for us, but Brehme equalized; even though Peter Shilton guessed right, it was out of his reach. Peter Beardsley was next in this game of nerves and he was successful, but Mattheus smashed his penalty past Shilton. Next it was David Platt: the keeper guessed right, but his shot made it into the corner. Aridle then made it 3–3 in the shoot-out.

Stuart Pearce, such a penalty expert at Nottingham Forest, hung his head in disbelief and disgust with himself as his fierce penalty shot struck the legs of goalkeeper Bodo Illgner. Thon made it worse for England by scoring his penalty. Finally, Chris Waddle smashed his penalty over the bar and it was all over for England.

Saturday 7 July   ENGLAND v. ITALY

In many ways, this was one of the best games of the

tournament, full of excitement, and I thoroughly enjoyed my part in it. It was unfortunate that we had to lose in a very close game but the match was full of atmosphere and it was one of the highlights of my career to be presented with a World Cup bronze medal.

After the match, Peter Shilton announced his retirement from international football and there must have been one or two more who felt that this was the end of their World Cup careers.

Sunday 8 July   We all realized that there had been phenomenal interest in our World Cup campaign back home but no one really imagined the volume of support that would greet us when we arrived back at Luton. It was frightening. I don't imagine for a minute that the security chiefs and police realized the sort of welcome we would get, as there were hardly sufficient numbers of security personnel to cope with the crowds. There must have been well over 100,000 people there, perhaps as many as 200,000. It took us four hours to crawl through the crowd on our open-top bus to the hotel. In many ways it was extremely dangerous. Yet it was such a lovely welcome, such a lovely day. However, I couldn't help worrying that there might be some sort of disaster because the crowd was not properly supervised. We had to lift a baby, still in the pram, on to the top of the bus. It couldn't have been more than a year old and had been brought there by its father, who no doubt did not expect such a crush. We had no way of knowing how many children and old people may have been hurt in the crowd. It took the edge off in a way but none the less we'll never forget our welcome back, nor will I ever forget the 1990 World Cup Finals in Italy.

Accompanied by Mark Wright, I flew from Luton to Manchester as we were both meeting up with our families to catch a flight the next morning for our holidays in Minorca. Ironically we had both booked the same resort on the same date, the seventh — in fact, our hotels were only a few miles apart — but we couldn't go out on time because our World Cup went on longer than we had both anticipated.

Mark and I watched the World Cup Final between holders Argentina and West Germany in a Manchester bar. It was a place Bryan Robson recommended, but there was a noticeable lack of atmosphere. The people were ecstatic when England were involved and doing so well, but now there was a 'couldn't care less' attitude. The Final was poor, and the whole occasion was an anti-climax for everyone, particularly for Mark and me. As we watched the Final we knew that England could easily have won the World Cup. The Argentinians were a waste of time, they were negative, and spoilers. England would easily have got their revenge for the World Cup Quarter-Final defeat four years ago in Mexico. West Germany knew that if they beat England in the Semi-Final they would have an outstanding chance of winning the World Cup by overcoming Argentina.

For the first time in a World Cup Final there was a sending off, and the Argentinians went one better and had two dismissed. Their substitute, Damian Pedro Monzon, was the first to go and make World Cup history after he tried to kick Klinsmann after 67 minutes. One could argue that the German over-reacted, that he wasn't touched, but the Argentinian certainly intended to hack him down, and a foul is a foul. The fact is, there were a lot of harsh refereeing decisions, and several unfair sendings off, but FIFA seemed intent on clamping down. West Germany's captain, Mattheus, played a superb through ball, Voeller was challenged and the referee awarded a penalty, the decision bringing fierce protests from the Argentinians, and Diego Maradona was almost begging the referee not to give it. Brehme made no mistake from the penalty spot. Once the second Argentinian was shown the red card for grabbing a German defender by the throat as he tried to waste time, the protests reached intolerable levels. Their manager, Bilardo, had to pull his players off the referee at the end when there were disgraceful scenes.

The Germans deserved to win, and it was lovely that England received the Fair Play trophy for the best disciplinary record even though I tried to spoil it by being one of only three England players booked. However, I would rather England had picked up the World Cup than the Fair Play award!

Chapter 16

The Future

I BELIEVE WE LEARNED a big lesson from the 1990 World Cup Finals. That was the versatility of English footballers, their adaptability to a sweeper system. This was a system that has proved so successful throughout Europe, particularly at international level, but one that we had shunned. It only went to prove our insularity. As I have already mentioned before the World Cup, I'm convinced the England manager never dreamed of playing the sweeper system but, once he tried it, it was proved conclusively that we have the players.

Our clubs have dabbled with the sweeper system and, because of the success of the England team, I'm convinced more will try it and I'm equally certain that Graham Taylor will persevere with it at international level. Graham Taylor has already played such a system at club level with Aston Villa and proved it can be effective, can give more scope not only at club level but in the international set-up. One of the important lessons of the World Cup was that we do possess players who can be flexible, who can adapt to the sweeper system, and it is worth experimenting with this at international level.

We have players of exceptional pace, such as Des Walker,

Mark Wright and Paul Parker, coupled with the emerging talents of Gary Pallister of Manchester United, to become one of the most complete defensive sweeper systems in the world. Yet, it is only in the last eight or ten years that our clubs have even considered playing such a system. It only goes to illustrate how stuck in its ways English football has become.

As far as the sweeper system goes, it has not been to our advantage, but in many ways I don't feel that it's been a bad thing to be stuck in our ways. While we have failed to adapt and modify our game to incorporate the sweeper system, the rest of the world have still been envious of many of the characteristics of English football. Everybody loves the English way and would like to incorporate our strengths of character and will to win. For that reason, we shouldn't change many of our attributes for anybody, including our approach to international football.

If we believe in ourselves, we can win the World Cup in America in 1994. Personally, I believe we can achieve that. My belief is that there are few teams now in the world who would confront us convinced that they can beat us, providing we put our minds to it. England only lost to West Germany on penalties, and might have easily beaten them, and would have certainly beaten Argentina in the Final. It might have been a cautious opening game against the Republic of Ireland but, as the World Cup progressed, we became more confident, more difficult to beat, and more assured.

The World Cup threw up some exceptional young players such as Paul Parker, who had gone to Italy as not much more than a squad member with little chance of being involved and finished the World Cup as a regular in defence. Mark Wright had an exceptional World Cup. Although he was almost two years in the international wilderness after the European Championships, he has forced himself into a position where he is assured of being a permanent fixture in England's defence right up until the next

World Cup Finals. David Platt was another who went to Italy on the fringe of the team and, although he actually took my place, I can't deny that he did a fabulous job and deservedly won the recognition as one of England's match winners. In fact, he looked as though he would score in every game he played for England.

Paul Gascoigne obviously came home a national hero, a larger than life character, a phenomenon in our lifetime. Remarkably, it will remain one of the unanswered questions of the World Cup: whether in fact he would have been in the England team had Neil Webb not damaged his Achilles tendon in Sweden on World Cup duty at the start of the World Cup season.

Neil Webb and Bryan Robson were the recognized first choice midfield pairing and there can be no doubt that Bobby Robson had it in mind to start them in the World Cup and probably stick by them right the way through the tournament. It is now impossible to tell whether Gazza would have been given his chance with two or three games to go before the World Cup finals, when the England manager would have been looking at players.

It's all ifs and buts now, but the fact is that Gazza had an exceptional World Cup. And, giving Bobby Robson the benefit of the doubt, perhaps he would have played Gazza, whether Neil Webb was fully fit or not, prior to the World Cup and the Spurs player's performances would have swayed him.

Everyone loves Gazza, me too! He deserves his World Cup recognition. What he doesn't deserve, and, no doubt, wants to avoid, is all the hype that has gone with it, that has driven him to the point of distraction in the first weeks of the new season. He has even admitted that he has been unable to sleep well with news reporters camped outside his house and stories about his private life in the papers.

Gazza has been built up as the next George Best and even

Players' Union leader Gordon Taylor has suggested that he should be a protected species, that we should all go easy on him to preserve his extraordinary talents. I've got a horrible feeling that Gazza's being built up, just like George Best was in the past, only to be knocked down.

I can't help worrying that if Gazza is booked, sent off or gets himself into trouble off the field that the knockers will be out again, criticizing him and, in the words of Bobby Robson, saying that they can't trust him.

Gazza faces a season that can either be the making of him or the breaking of him. It won't make him a better player because he already possesses all the natural ability that any player would want. It is how he copes as a person that will be so interesting.

Personally, I believe that he possesses the strength of character to come through yet another trial, possibly even another ordeal. I love to have Gazza around in an England squad, where he is the life and soul of the party. He got up to too many pranks to recall any specific ones, he was always twitching and on the move, he could never keep still and he was always saying what he thought out loud. Half the time he doesn't really mean the sort of things he says or gets up to. When Bobby Robson was giving some of his talks it was like being back at school, with Gazza showing his nerves, twitching about and the England manager putting him in his place like a naughty little boy.

It is imperative that referees understand him and treat him carefully. I'm not saying he should be wrapped in cotton wool or allowed to get away with anything, but a lot of his bookings are for dissent, unnecessary cautions. However, it is too easy to write all this off: that referees are picking on him and that decisions are going against him. True, referees could be a little more tolerant but it is really up to Gazza to control himself, particularly verbally.

179

He is certainly not an angel! He can be a hard player, and a couple of times he surprised me in the World Cup at how well he got stuck in. Some people have compared him to Dave Mackay and he does have the guts to go into the tackle as well as demand the ball to display his enormous skills. Quite simply, he cannot have it all his own way. You cannot expect to be a great tackler and not mistime your challenges on occasions and get on the wrong side of referees. The important thing is to keep your mouth shut and not back-chat officials and needlessly go into the book for dissent.

There are many experts who are convinced that Spurs are now genuine title contenders because of the influence of Paul Gascoigne and also not forgetting Gary Lineker. But Spurs came third last season and have virtually the same set of players that they have had for the past two years. Just because Gazza has had a great World Cup, people are starting to believe that Spurs will win the League Championship. I don't want to disappoint them, but it doesn't quite work out like that. Once again, I have no qualms about fancying ourselves for the Championship. If somebody comes above us in the League, then they will win it.

Of course, Spurs must come into the reckoning, but the London club I most fancy are Arsenal. They have purchased three exceptional players during the summer to increase their strength in depth. I would not be surprised if Manchester United, after collecting the FA Cup, did not mount a serious challenge along with Tottenham and also fellow Merseysiders, Everton. Although Everton have had their problems with a number of players wanting to leave Goodison, they still have a terrific squad of players.

I sense great expectations for the new football season based on England's successes in the World Cup. There is a stimulation for League football and that is encouraging. But there is now a thirst for success at international level and I sincerely hope that England's new manager Graham Taylor can provide it.

Graham Taylor is the ideal choice as the new England manager and I'm not just saying that for ulterior motives. He comes across as a serious, genuine man. For many years, Brian Clough has been dubbed the People's Choice, but I firmly believe that Graham Taylor is a man of the people as well and I'm sure he will provide the supporters with what they want and communicate with them on their level.

I have worked with Graham Taylor in the past with the England B team. I've always found him full of good ideas and I have enjoyed the limited association I've had with him.

It is interesting to see that he has made several innovations right at the start of his England career, one of which is joining training sessions with the clubs. Unfortunately, I'm not convinced that he will learn that much, particularly when he comes to Liverpool. I think he will be shocked when he comes to Anfield; in fact, I don't think he will know what's hit him. Liverpool have their own way of doing things, both on and off the pitch. Everything is recorded: all the coaches from Steve Highway, through to Phil Thompson and first team coach Ronnie Moran write everything down. I'm sure Ronnie Moran's records over the past twenty years would be worth a bob or two – in fact, they'd be worth a fortune. Basically, Kenny Dalglish simply picks the team. He may get opinions from a variety of people and he might consult all his coaches, everyone will get their heads together, but Kenny is very much his own man: he buys the players he wants and selects the team and the tactics he wants, depending on the match. I'm sure Graham would enjoy coming to Anfield but I can't believe he would learn much.

However, in theory, his idea of going to the clubs, trying to get close to the players and the managers, is a sound idea. In the past, the England manager has seemed a little aloof: very few people knew him and only saw him when they would meet up for England squad sessions and matches. To see him turn up personally to take club training sessions would bring him a little closer to some of the players. There can be no harm in that, only positive vibes. It shows that Graham Taylor wants people to feel part of the England set-up and it seems to me as if he wants to treat the England international scene like a club set-up and that would only win my approval.

He has chosen Lawrie McMenemy as his assistant, and to many that is a surprise appointment, but every manager has certain people whom he trusts and wants to bring in. I know little about Lawrie McMenemy on a personal level but his record has been impressive, although he left Sunderland on a sour note. But there has been nothing to criticize Graham Taylor for on his judgement so far, and if he didn't believe in Lawrie McMenemy he wouldn't have chosen him.

The appointment of Graham Taylor has only increased my belief that the England team can build on what was achieved in Italy and go on to win the World Cup in 1994. I'm convinced that Graham Taylor can cope with the extraordinary pressures of being England manager. Bobby Robson coped in his own way despite taking a lot of stick. He always seemed prepared to get on with it and co-operate even with those who were his chief critics. The only way for an England manager is to be open and honest and, of course, pick the best team and get the right results.

It has been widely felt that several members of the 1990 World Cup squad will be over the hill by 1994. That may be the case, and the new England manager can only retain some of those senior players if they are performing well enough. Sometimes it can be a mistake to discard players of vast experience too early. You cannot dismiss such a wealth of experience that players like Bryan Robson and Gary Lineker possess. If they are playing as well as anybody, if not better than some, in the country, then they ought to be picked. Peter Shilton and Terry Butcher have announced their retirement from international football, but there are several senior members of the squad in Italy who can still be very useful in leading England to the European Championships in Sweden in 1992.

The European Championships can also be a big stepping stone for young players emerging on the international scene, helping to groom them and providing them with vital experience for the next World Cup. Perhaps the biggest problem England faces is to discover the new strikers for 1994. I'm sure the young players will emerge, but at the moment there is still none better than Gary Lineker.

With strikers you sometimes have to stick by them even if they are going through a lean spell at club level. The international manager has to say, 'Well, he has done well for me I will continue to play him.' That is not to say that an England manager should not take note of players' current form. Steve Bull is certainly worthy of more of a chance than he's been given so far and there is a lot expected of Southampton's Matthew Le Tissier – he is a possibility, but I wouldn't class him as an out-and-out striker, more of a floater between midfield and attack.

The future for football certainly looks good, particularly with the World Cup generating such excitement, and it seems that everybody loves football again. Football has a tendency to go in stages, and there was a time, not so long ago, when the game was discredited in the eyes of the public, mainly because of the problems with hooliganism. The England team in the World Cup Finals has helped to convince so many people to have confidence in our football again and that might provide an upsurge in attendances, with the graph going steadily upwards in the last few years. The government and the football authorities have done their bit in helping to curb violence, particularly inside stadiums, and I don't think they could do much more in this sphere. There has been an emphasis placed on families and family sections and I would like to see this extended. There is every incentive for spectators to return to the game and watch their favourite team in a greater degree of comfort.

It is becoming more expensive to watch football and that is reflected in the cost of living, but I don't think even the ordinary man in the street will want to miss out on his football, irrespective of the cost. I just hope the prices don't become ridiculously high, even though I accept that football is relatively inexpensive compared to other forms of entertainment such as theatre.

Facilities are bound to improve, with the government insisting on all-seater stadiums. Clubs have become big business, the game money orientated, and it needs to be to foot the huge bill for all-seater stadiums. Football is still basically a working-class sport and I would hate for the game to be out of the price range of the ordinary working man. However, the game is changing rapidly with the advent of executive boxes which is a far cry from how the game was viewed twenty years ago. But there is an increase in the number of people who want to watch the sport in a degree of luxury and they can afford to buy the executive suites.

Yet, I'm still convinced that the working-class man is prepared to save all week and deprive himself of some luxuries, if necessary, to ensure that he can afford to watch his favourite team on a Saturday. There is more opportunity to stay at home and watch football on either BBC or ITV, and now on one of the two satellite TV stations. But nothing can replace going out and watching a match 'live' on a Saturday afternoon.

When one analyses the future of the game, trying to assess in which direction it might be heading, it perturbs me that the Football League have decided to switch back from twenty clubs to twenty-two. It just seems to me that the League have not learnt their lesson. Twenty-two clubs mean that there will be too many games again in our domestic football. We should be seeking quality, not quantity. There should be more opportunity for England get-togethers and preparation for vital England matches, and the players should be allowed more breathing space, more time to recover from injuries. It just seems that our game never stops. On the Continent there is a mid-winter break for around three weeks at Christmas time, but in our game that is the most important period, especially financially in terms of attendances. Regrettably, our game seems to be focused on finances. I was surprised that my own club Liverpool voted in favour of returning to a 22-club First Division. I just cannot agree with their philosophy but I stress that's a personal view.

It is no doubt that Liverpool's stance has been encouraged by UEFA's refusal to allow the club back into Europe when it reopened its doors to English clubs. At least it's a start, with Manchester United and Aston Villa, but UEFA have insisted that the extra ban remains on Liverpool. I would hope that the barrier comes down as far as Liverpool is concerned next season.

I'm convinced that the rest of Europe miss the English clubs and Liverpool in particular. I don't believe that any team could be classed as the true champions of Europe unless they've played the English clubs, especially Liverpool. AC Milan would love to pit their skills against us, and no one on the Continent can hide from the fact that their crown would be false until they played Liverpool.

Players must share the responsibility for the well-being of the game for future generations and, in this respect, our union leader, Gordon Taylor, is playing a very vital part. However, I do have a criticism in that the players should become more involved in the decision-making of the Players' Union, and there should be many more mass meetings and dialogues with the players to sort out the problems. Bruce Grobbelaar is our PFA representative but it seems that we just pay our fees and we don't hear too much of our own union's activities till we're voting for the player of the year. Our representatives, no doubt, have numerous meetings but I feel that the grass roots should come in closer contact with Gordon Taylor, letting him know exactly how they feel about vital issues.

Discipline on the field is a vital area for convincing the government and the football authorities that players can behave themselves and pass on a good image to the spectators. I can't for the life of me see how hugging and kissing can cause any trouble, despite what some people might think. If you cannot get overexcited about scoring a goal then you should pack the game in. However, I do agree that climbing on fences and making gestures to the fans can be provocative. But there is no reason why players can't celebrate goals however they want: falling to their knees, giving the sign of the Cross, or dancing around the corner flag as one Cameroon player did in the World Cup. People love all that; the game is about entertainment, it's supposed to make you smile, and I don't mind it because it is doing no one any harm, it's only a bit of fun.

I would like to see one fundamental change and that is a British Cup competition. The top eight Scottish clubs and the top eight English clubs in a knock-out tournament would be an absolute winner, and I'm sure it would capture the imagination of the public and there would be full houses.

After the exploits of the England team in Italy, we shall all be looking forward to the 1994 World Cup Finals in America. There's been a lot of speculation that the Americans won't be able to stage the World Cup Finals because there is little support for the game in their own country. I don't agree. They have such fantastic facilities and they know how to put on an event. I'm sure the game will catch on again, inspired by the prospect of staging the World Cup Finals. If the Americans can't get it right then who can?

However, I hope they keep adverts out of their TV coverage. I would hate to see the game divided up into four quarters to fit into lucrative advert slots on peak-time TV. I'm as much against that as I am opposed to stopping the game to have video reruns of major incidents – then the game could last as long as four hours because I'd be complaining about every decision!

I have always liked to think there would be a future for me in the game when I finish as a player, and initially I'd like to remain in the profession as a coach, hoping to progress into management. I know Kenny Dalglish went straight from being a player into management, and into one of the top jobs in the country, if not the top job, but he is an exception. I can't see myself doing anything else apart from a life in football and, of course, one day I'd love to be Liverpool manager. I'm sure that even Kenny Dalglish didn't imagine when he was at the same stage of his career as I am at now that he would be Liverpool manager.

It's one thing saying that you'd like to be Liverpool manager, it's a vastly different thing actually doing it. You'd have to believe in fairy-tales, but you never know. Quite simply, I'd like to be a coach and then a manager, and then I'll see how far that takes me. Of course, I wouldn't say no to being Liverpool manager! But there have been plenty in the past who thought that they would join the Liverpool line of succession, such as Phil Neal and John Toshack, but they have yet to make it. I do approve of the system at Anfield of appointing from within but, although the job looks easy, particularly with the squad of players at the manager's disposal, it's far from being that simple and in reality it's a very tough job. To pursue my ambition of moving into coaching and management I'm taking a coaching course next summer.

Football has provided me with a good living, but it's not just the financial rewards that have attracted me, but all the trimmings, such as the travelling, and I would miss it enormously if I failed to stay in the game. Just ask Kenny Dalglish – even though he's got one of the top managerial jobs in world football, deep down he would still love to be a player and he misses that. I've discovered so many people who have told me how much they've regretted it when they have left the game. I'm sure I will come in to the coaching side with some good ideas; I've certainly worked under some outstanding managers and you're bound to pick up some tips from them.

However, my immediate ambitions are to keep on playing, and play on for as long as I possibly can. Every season I now regard as a bonus and it gives me even greater encouragement to produce my best. I'm sure it's a question of the older you get the more you appreciate that you're still in the game as a player. I'll be around 32/33 by the time of the next World Cup in America in 1994, and I don't believe I'll be too old. The game is really about fitness and, if I'm physically still in good shape, I hope I would still be considered for the next World Cup. But first I have to impress the new manager Graham Taylor and that's what I aim to do.

FOR THE BEST IN PAPERBACKS, LOOK FOR THE

In every corner of the world, on every subject under the sun, Penguin represents quality and variety – the very best in publishing today.

For complete information about books available from Penguin – including Puffins, Penguin Classics and Arkana – and how to order them, write to us at the appropriate address below. Please note that for copyright reasons the selection of books varies from country to country.

In the United Kingdom: Please write to *Dept E.P., Penguin Books Ltd, Harmondsworth, Middlesex, UB7 0DA.*

If you have any difficulty in obtaining a title, please send your order with the correct money, plus ten per cent for postage and packaging, to *PO Box No 11, West Drayton, Middlesex*

In the United States: Please write to *Dept BA, Penguin, 299 Murray Hill Parkway, East Rutherford, New Jersey 07073*

In Canada: Please write to *Penguin Books Canada Ltd, 2801 John Street, Markham, Ontario L3R 1B4*

In Australia: Please write to the *Marketing Department, Penguin Books Australia Ltd, P.O. Box 257, Ringwood, Victoria 3134*

In New Zealand: Please write to the *Marketing Department, Penguin Books (NZ) Ltd, Private Bag, Takapuna, Auckland 9*

In India: Please write to *Penguin Overseas Ltd, 706 Eros Apartments, 56 Nehru Place, New Delhi, 110019*

In the Netherlands: Please write to *Penguin Books Netherlands B.V., Postbus 195, NL–1380AD Weesp*

In West Germany: Please write to *Penguin Books Ltd, Friedrichstrasse 10–12, D–6000 Frankfurt/Main 1*

In Spain: Please write to *Alhambra Longman S.A., Fernandez de la Hoz 9, E–28010 Madrid*

In Italy: Please write to *Penguin Italia s.r.l., Via Como 4, I-20096 Pioltello (Milano)*

In France: Please write to *Penguin Books Ltd, 39 Rue de Montmorency, F-75003 Paris*

In Japan: Please write to *Longman Penguin Japan Co Ltd, Yamaguchi Building, 2–12–9 Kanda Jimbocho, Chiyoda-Ku, Tokyo 101*

BIOGRAPHY AND AUTOBIOGRAPHY IN PENGUIN

My Father's Island   Johanna Angermeyer

In 1935 Johanna's father Hans and his four brothers had fled from Nazi Germany to the Galapagos Islands. Then he died, and his daughter travelled 2,000 miles to the enchanted isles he had loved – there to piece together the story of her parents' incredible lives, their enforced separation and her father's tragic death.

The Secret Lives of Trebitsch Lincoln   Bernard Wasserstein

Trebitsch Lincoln was Member of Parliament, international spy, right-wing revolutionary, Buddhist monk – and this century's most extraordinary conman. 'An utterly improbable story … a biographical scoop' – *Guardian*

Tolstoy   A. N. Wilson

'One of the best biographies of our century' – Leon Edel. 'All his skills as a writer, his fire as a critic, his insight as a novelist and his experience of life have come together in this subject' – Peter Levi in the *Independent*

Brian Epstein: The Man Who Made the Beatles   Ray Coleman

'An excellent biography of Brian Epstein, the lonely, gifted man whose artistic faith and bond with the Beatles never wavered – and whose recognition of genius created a cultural era, even though it destroyed him' – *Mail on Sunday*

Backcloth   Dirk Bogarde

The final volume of Dirk Bogarde's autobiography is not about his acting years but about Dirk Bogarde the man and the people and events that have shaped his life and character. All are remembered with affection, nostalgia and characteristic perception and eloquence.

Searching for Bobby Fischer   Fred Waitzkin

Since Bobby Fischer retired from chess in 1975 Americans have been searching for a successor. Fred Waitzkin describes how he helped his gifted son Josh become a leading contender. 'A terrific book for fathers, sons, chess players and the general reader' – Tom Stoppard